WHAT
ABOUT
DIVINE
HEALING?

WHAT ABOUT DIVINE HEALING?

A Study of Christian Healing

FaithQuestions SERIES

Susan Sonnenday Vogel

ABINGDON PRESS
NASHVILLE

WHAT ABOUT DIVINE HEALING?
A Study of Christian Healing

Copyright © 2004 by Abingdon Press

This book is printed on acid-free, elemental chlorine-free paper.

ISBN: 0-687-00068-8
ISBN: 978-068700068-5

07 08 09 10 11 12 13—10 9 8 7 6 5 4 3 2

MANUFACTURED IN THE UNITED STATES OF AMERICA

For Linda,
who is teaching me God's healing—
beyond all I can ask or imagine

CONTENTS

HOW TO USE
WHAT ABOUT DIVINE HEALING?
A STUDY OF CHRISTIAN HEALING

WHAT ABOUT DIVINE HEALING? A STUDY OF CHRISTIAN HEALING recognizes and celebrates God as the source of healing as it explores healing and what healing means in the Bible, in Christian tradition, and in contemporary culture. It examines ways God heals individuals and communities through such resources as prayer, worship, ritual, and relationships. This study is intended to help people reclaim hope in God's sustaining love and power as they explore Christian views of healing. The book is designed for use in any of three settings: (1) adult Sunday school, (2) weekday adult groups, and (3) retreat settings. It can also provide a meaningful resource for private study and reflection. You will find endnotes to direct you to other resources that will enrich your learning.

Sunday School: WHAT ABOUT DIVINE HEALING? may be used on Sunday mornings as a short-term, seven-week study. Sunday morning groups generally last 45 to 60 minutes. If your group would like to go into greater depth, you can divide the chapters and do the study for longer than seven weeks.

Weekday Study: If you use WHAT ABOUT DIVINE HEALING? in a weekday study, we recommend 90-minute sessions. Participants should prepare ahead by reading the content of the chapter and choosing one activity for deeper reflection and study. A group leader may wish to assign these activities. You may also wish to use some of the books included in the endnotes of each chapter.

Retreat Study: You may wish to use WHAT ABOUT DIVINE HEALING? in a more intense study like a weekend retreat. Distribute the books at least two weeks in advance. Locate and provide additional media resources and reference materials, such as hymn books, Bibles, Bible dictionaries and commentaries, and books listed in the endnotes. If possible, you may wish to provide a computer with Internet capabilities onsite. Tell participants to read WHAT ABOUT DIVINE HEALING? before the retreat. Begin on Friday with an evening meal or refreshments followed by gathering time and worship. Do the activities in Chapter One. Cover Chapters Two, Three, Four, Five, and Six on Saturday. Develop a schedule that includes time for breaks, for meals, and for personal reflection on various topics in the chapters. Cover Chapter Seven on Sunday. End the retreat with closing worship on Sunday afternoon.

Leader/Learner Helps

Leader/learner helps are located in boxes near the relevant main text. They offer a variety of discussion and reflection activities. Include both the Gathering and Closing worship activities for each chapter, and choose from among the other leader/learner helps to fit the time frame you have chosen for your group.

The activities in the leader/learner helps meet the needs of a variety of personalities and ways of learning. They are designed to stimulate both solitary reflection and group discussion. An interactive and informal environment will encourage a dynamic interchange of ideas and demonstrate the value of diverse perspectives. While the readings may be done in the group, reading outside of the session will enrich individual reflection and group discussion.

Most of the chapters include a list of further research options in the endnotes. You will enrich your learning by reading one or more of the listed resources in the endnotes and by taking extra time for Internet research.

The Role of the Group Leader

A group leader facilitates gathering and closing worship, organizes the group for each session, monitors the use of time so that adequate attention is given to all major points of the chapter, and fosters an atmosphere of mutual respect and Christian caring. The leader should participate fully in the study as both learner and leader. The same person may lead all the sessions, or each session may have a different leader.

INTRODUCTION

"What do you want me to do for you?" (Mark 10:51)

A foolish question, they must have thought. The answer was clear to all. Bartimaeus was blind. He was calling loudly, persistently, to the one whom the people said could bring healing: "Jesus, Son of David, have mercy on me!" Jesus called in return; and, the story tells us, Bartimaeus "sprang up and came to Jesus." Then Jesus asked this question:

"What do you want me to do for you?"

Scholars show us many ways to study and understand this conversation and the events that follow. But first, what might we discover if we enter this conversation and hear this question? What might our hearts answer when Jesus asks,

"What do you want me to do for you?"

I want comfort for the ache of grief that lives beside every joy. My neighbor prays, and I with him, for relief from AIDS-related illnesses that are filling and breaking down his body. My congregation craves a good ending to the hurt of betrayal. Together we ask for an ending of wars and rumors of war.

"What do you want me to do for you?"

A woman approaching her middle years wails with anguish at the debilitating memory of abuse by her brother many years ago. My brother in Christ has built an unyielding wall around his understanding of Scripture and will not welcome his sisters as colleagues in ministry. A nearby community of faith opens its doors to invite the neighborhood to worship—to

11

sing their beloved hymns and to hear their stirring anthems. They are puzzled when visitors do not return.

"What do you want me to do for you?"

Each of us listens to this question, and our hearts are filled with answers. We stand within our communities of faith and look upon our sisters and brothers, and more answers pour out of us. We step back and survey our country, our world, and still more answers overflow.

To begin to answer Jesus' question is to begin a conversation about healing.
To begin to look at
      that for which we ache and
      that which we know brings suffering to others
      is to begin a long and difficult conversation about healing.
It is long and it is difficult because there are many different kinds of healing and a myriad of understandings of healing. People of faith look to many resources to come to adequate and faithful understandings of what healing is and are called to discern what our understandings mean for faithful living.

It is a long and difficult conversation. And, the conversation matters. A few years ago, two colleagues chose those words to title their book—*The Conversation Matters: Why United Methodists Should Talk with One Another.* In our study and teaching and learning, all people of faith can profit from the wisdom that these two dedicated Christian scholars offer to us. Hal Knight and Don Saliers write out of their Wesleyan tradition and draw upon particular language and practices that grew out of the ministry and writing of John Wesley. The spirit of their work and the guidelines that emerge from it, however, can provide the grounding for conversation among those from many communities of faith. United Methodists are not the only ones about whom it can be said that "we stand in a tradition that honors communal theological thinking." [1]

This conversation about healing is a long and difficult one, and the conversation matters. It *matters* that we engage in this hard work because God's people seek healing and do not agree about what healing means. We ache for wholeness in our bodies and in our relationships, and we are not sure what it looks like, what it feels like, what it is. All of us yearn to know where to look for sources of healing, and we hear conflicting directions that promise to guide us. Some of us are in despair and confusion, for others have known healing and we have not. I have life and my child has died.

And the *conversation* matters—our conversations with our sisters and brothers, with resources with which we have been blessed, with ourselves within our hearts and minds, and with our God, who is present in every conversation.

How we *do* the conversation matters. Our commitment to engage with one another *matters* because no one of us has all of God's wisdom. I often paraphrase Catherine of Siena: God could have made us perfect, but God chose not to make us perfect so we would need one another. Our willingness to speak to and listen to one another *matters* because our Scripture and tradition show how God consistently brings words of truth to us through other persons. St. John of the Cross wrote: "[God] does not want us to bestow entire credence upon [God's] communications, . . . until they pass through the human channel of the mouth of [another person]." [2]

The spirit in which we engage one another *matters* because we are dealing with complex, multifaceted questions; and the possibility of new understanding multiplies as we build upon one another's insights. Knight and Saliers help us see there is a myth of only "two positions" on issues we address. As we engage the complex and difficult dimensions of divine healing, we are likely to discover multiple new understandings and an expansion of our questions. [3] Our engagement of opposing views *matters* because it is sometimes in the collision of opposites that a new possibility emerges. Mary Parker Follett said that even "our 'opponents' are our co-creators, for they have something to give which we have not." [4]

Our willingness to touch heart as well as mind *matters* because much of what shapes our understanding of healing has come to us in images and stories and nonverbal learning. What reason has not put into us, reason is seldom able to change.

Our persistence in wrestling with the questions *matters* because we may not find "the answer" or resolution in the way we anticipate. As one who is providing the text for the beginning of this conversation, I have been encouraged in my task by words of one philosopher/psychologist:

No writer writes out of [one's] having found the answer to the problem; [one] writes rather out of [one's] having the problem and *wanting* a solution. The solution consists not of a resolution. It consists of the *deeper and wider dimension of consciousness to which the writer is carried by virtue of [one's] wrestling with that problem.* [5]

13

Such wrestling offers to us a deeper and wider dimension of consciousness, to which we are carried by virtue of having wrestled. I pray that is also the rich harvest of our conversation that issues from the writing of this text. That deeper and wider consciousness may hold paradoxes and ambiguities that challenge the logical parts of our minds. But, warned a wise priest, "Beware of synthesists in sheep's clothing. They are out to rob you of the richness of multiple and contradictory truths."[6]

The conversation matters, and how we *do* the conversation matters. When our work together comes to an end, I trust that we will have discovered new questions to ask; that our curiosities will be leading us to pursue learning only touched in these pages; and that we will have entered into a continuing, lifelong conversation. I will bring stories—my own and ones that have touched my life. You will bring your stories. Together we will weave new stories in the presence of the One whose story surrounds and shapes us. I pray our work together with divine healing may be a conversation that lives within our awareness of God's healing presence, that invites each of us into searching and healing engagement with one another, and that moves us to a deeper and wider consciousness of what God's healing is and how it forms our living and dying.

Notes

1. Henry H. Knight III and Don E. Saliers, *The Conversation Matters: Why United Methodists Should Talk with One Another* (Nashville: Abingdon Press, 1999), page 12. Knight and Saliers wrote this book in response to the current polarizations the authors saw in their own denomination as well as in others, polarizations that call for divine healing. The first half of the book describes the "what" of the conversation—the place of doctrine in the Wesleyan tradition in particular. The second part addresses the "how," with chapters on "Civility: Speaking the Truth in Love" and "Dialogue: Seeking the Truth in Christian Conversation." The book offers an invaluable framework for any conversation—particularly those that will be long and difficult. The United Methodist Council of Bishops chose it for their own study and recommended it to others in the church who have been addressing difficult questions.

2. St. John of the Cross, *The Collected Works of St. John of the Cross* (Washington DC: ICS Publications, Institute of Carmelite Studies, 1979), page 182.

3. *The Conversation Matters,* page 75.

4. Mary Parker Follett, *Creative Experience* (New York: Longmans, Green and Company, 1924), page 174.

5. Rollo May, *Love and Will* (New York: W. W. Norton and Company, 1969), pages 170–71.

6. Thomas Woodward, *Turning Things Upside Down: A Theological Workbook* (New York: Seabury Press, 1975), page 10.

CHAPTER 1
"I CAME THAT THEY
MAY HAVE LIFE . . ."

What does "healing" mean?

Focus: This chapter explores definitions of divine healing and offers opportunities to identify God's healing in stories involving the absence of a physical cure, grief associated with loss, and brokenness in communities.

Gathering
    Sing together two or three times "Come and Fill Our Hearts."[1] Then join together in prayer:

Center us down, O God, until in our deepest soul we kneel, quietly, waitfully, reverently. Deliver us from the world for these brief moments, so that we may meet thee undistractedly, and confirm the bond that binds us to thee. Then in thy presence help us to reorder our minds and hearts, bringing before thee one by one our loved ones, our hopes and fears, our great joys and our ill-admitted sins, until we see with thine eyes and love with thy grace.[2]

    After a few moments of silence, lift concerns for healing that are on your hearts. All respond in prayer: *We bring this care before you.*
    Close with these words: *Help us to reorder our minds and hearts, until we see with your eyes and love with your grace. Amen.*

The Conversation Begins

Our exploration of divine healing begins with a conversation in Mark 10:46-52, which tells a specific story about divine healing. In the story, Bartimaeus, who is blind, shouted to Jesus, "Jesus, Son of David, have mercy on me!" Jesus stood still and asked Bartimaeus a question:

"What do you want me to do for you?"

Jesus asked this question of Bartimaeus. He asks it of you and of me. It is a question that implicitly acknowledges that healing can mean many things. How we answer the question carries our understanding of divine healing.

"What do you want me to do for you?"

I anticipated several of my answers in the introductory pages. In 1990, my 23-year-old son died in an automobile accident. What did I want Jesus to do? At the beginning, as I watched Mark lie in a coma, I wanted Jesus to make him well. I wept and begged and bargained. When we grew clear that his brain was badly damaged, and he was no longer the Mark we had known, I promised to love whoever the Mark was who survived. Then, finally and with anguished reluctance, I put him in God's hands, where, of course, he had always been. In the years since, I have wanted Jesus to bring comfort for my grief, to heal the longing that lives beside each joy.

During the past five years, I have watched my friend William grow gaunt and despairing as he fought the disease and infection invading his AIDS-weakened body. Often feeling alone in what he saw to be a part-nered world, he grew weary in his heart. Today he is deciding to end the fight. "No more medications," he has declared.

In those first years, I prayed that Jesus would protect William's body from disease. New medications were working for many; he could have a long, full life. But what he wanted Jesus to do for him was to bring him someone to love—someone who would love him as one, now gone, had loved him. Today I want peace for him—the kind that only Jesus can give. That is what I want Jesus to do today.

In recent months, I have been blessed and challenged to help provide pastoral leadership for a grieving congregation. One whom they loved acted in a way that hurt many and damaged trust. Some felt betrayed;

others, angry. All are grieving. What do we all want Jesus to do for us? We want a new beginning, a renewal of trust, a measure of good growing out of the hurt.

And in these months and years of war and rumors of war, we want Jesus to bring strife to an end. We want an end to conflict in the Middle East and the threats that emerge from those hate-filled divisions. We want the nations of Africa and Asia, South and Central America, to find peaceful processes for addressing their differences. In our own land, we want what we pledge: "liberty and justice for all." Come, Lord Jesus.

> Read Mark 10:41-46. Imagine that Jesus has just entered the room and asked you, "What do you want me to do for you? for your family and friends? for your community and our world?" Take a few moments to write answers. Share your answers with two or three others. Are there any commonalities among you? From where do you imagine the differences come? What answers, if any, describe what you want for others that they may not want for themselves?

For the woman whose anguish reaches a wail as she weeps in my office, I want justice and the assurance in her soul that Jesus hears her. For my brother in Christ who would turn me and my sisters away from our calling to ministry, I want a new heart for discerning God's word. For the congregation who seeks in earnest to reach its community, and treasures passionately its own traditions and practices, I want Jesus to widen their circle of imagination.

> How do you define *healing*? How do you define *divine healing*? Make a group list of your definitions. Save the list for use near the end of the session.

"What do you want me to do for you?"

What are your answers?
In relation to yourself?
In relation to your community?
In relation to our world?

To begin to answer Jesus' question is to begin a conversation about healing.
To begin to look at
that for which we ache and
that which we know brings suffering to others
is to begin a long and difficult conversation about healing.

17

"I Came That They May Have Life . . ."

When we imagine Jesus asking us a question about what we want him to do for us, we respond with our own answers. Now, through the Gospel of John, Jesus tells us what he came to do for us. "I came that they may have life, and have it abundantly" (John 10:10b). He has come that *we* may have life, and have it abundantly—"in all its fullness" (NEB), or, in the paraphrase of Eugene Peterson, so we can have "real and eternal life, more and better life than [we] ever dreamed of" (THE MESSAGE).[3]

When I imagine Jesus asking his question of me, and I answer in the words that pour out of my heart, I am saying what I believe is wrong or broken or diseased within me, in others, and in our world. My answer also points, by implication, toward what I believe is right and good and whole, toward what I believe God wants for me and for us.

In John's Gospel, Jesus says to you and me what *his* answer is to the question. What he wants to do for us is bring life, abundant life, in all its fullness, real and eternal, more and better than we could ever dream.

As we begin our conversation about healing, we understand that it will be long and difficult, for we come with many different experiences of what is wrong and broken. We are looking for a vision of what is right and good, what God wants for us. Now we hear that God in Jesus Christ wants us to have life abundant and full, more and better than we could ever dream. Is Jesus offering an alternative vision for us? Is he saying to us, "Look at all that you believe is wrong and broken. Look at what *you* believe is good and right and whole. Look at it all in light of the life *I* bring—a full and abundant life, more and better than you can ever imagine."

People of faith through the centuries have offered many differing understandings of what abundant life looks like. We bring differing understandings because we have differing experiences of what is wrong and broken. But Jesus may be saying to all of us, "Whatever it is that you believe is good, what I have to bring far exceeds all you can imagine." Is that not the story that weaves through our salvation history? One surprising chapter follows another, and we see our God as one whose power works within us "to accomplish abundantly far more than all we can ask or imagine" (Ephesians 3:20).

Consult a dictionary of the Bible and begin a word study of *healing*. You will discover, for example, that some Hebrew words that are translated "to heal" and "health" come from the root we know in the noun *shalom*. Among its meanings are: be complete or sound, uninjured; to make whole or good,

18

restore, make safe, complete; quiet, tranquility, contentment; peace with others or friendship; peace with God; peace from war. In the New Testament there are words for *health* and *healing* related to *save* or *salvation*. *Healing* in the biblical tradition consistently involves one's relationship with God. In the Old Testament illness was often understood as the result of sin or disobedience, and health and wholeness was understood to emerge from one's obedience to God's way. Jesus understood that God's desire was for human wholeness and salvation. Illness was often associated with evil that upset or distorted the human wholeness desired by God.

We believe we know the healing we seek—for ourselves, for others, for our world. We may be clear about the meaning of the healing for which we pray. We also may be surprised when our lives are re-shaped in ways far beyond all we can ask or imagine.

As I have read the story of Bartimaeus (Mark 10:46-52), and as I imagine that I am blind, it seems obvious that what I want is to "see again." Healing means regaining my sight. Then, as the Gospel of Mark tells the story, I discover that Jesus brings something else. I do regain my sight. Suddenly, though, that is not

> **For Further Information**
> Look up *healing* in a Bible dictionary like *The Interpreter's Dictionary of the Bible*. Read through the article to discover the many nuances of *healing* in the Bible. How does your reading inform your understanding of healing?

the center of my story. Something else is happening. Something is happening between Jesus and me far beyond what I had asked—or could possibly dream.

I ask to see again, and Jesus is telling me that my faith is making me well. It has already made me well. I can see, and I rejoice. I am overwhelmed by my good fortune. How can I understand? Jesus is talking to me about my faith. What is this faith? From where did it come? It seems as if it came in those moments when I heard Jesus' voice, as I called to him, and as he answered me.

My faith? It welled up within my heart as Jesus called me. What did I do? I heard that voice, and then I called. He was the source of all that happened; and yet, he says it was my faith that made me well. More is happening to me now than seeing again. Jesus has stirred within my heart something that was not here before. I am also well. I am well far beyond

> See the film or read the play *Children of a Lesser God.* In what ways does it challenge some of our assumptions about "disabilities"? What does it teach us about what healing can mean?

seeing again—though that would be miracle enough. I sense that my wellness will be always tied to him, and I must be with him. I must follow him along the way he is going. If I am Bartimaeus, I think I know what healing means. Then I am surprised at the way in which Jesus works in me that I may have abundant life—far beyond all that I have ever dreamed. Healing involves more than the physical. It also involves my relationship with Jesus Christ.

Divine Healing in Many Forms

What is healing? What does healing mean? What does it look like?

Jesus asks, "What do you want me to do for you?" Our answers flow out of our hearts as we look at what we believe is broken or wrong or diseased within or around us. We want Jesus to heal—to right the wrong, mend what is broken, bring health to what we know as disease. Like Bartimaeus, we may discover that what we want does not begin to encompass what Jesus wants for us.

Margaret Kim Peterson writes tenderly of the last chapter of her husband's life. Hyung Goo had known much brokenness; misery, depression, and poor judgments grew to be familiar companions. Then, for several years, he lived with HIV/AIDS and the diseases that came with it until his body grew weak. As the community around them prayed for healing, it was difficult to know what anyone expected. Could the virus disappear? Would his strength return? The virus did not disappear. Hyung Goo's body did not grow stronger. Although he was not cured, he did know healing. His depression lifted, and "he was present and open, able to love and to be loved . . ."[4]

> In a way as undeniable as it was mysterious, Hyung Goo was more whole when he died than he had been at any other time in his life. It was not the sort of healing that we had hoped or asked for. How could we have asked for it, *when we couldn't even imagine it?* [italics added].[5]

"What do you want me to do for you?"

How could we have asked for it,

"I came that they may have life, and have it abundantly."

when we couldn't even imagine it?

What will healing look like? Who can imagine it?

Since I began writing, my lonely friend William, who decided to stop taking his medication, has died. "Passed peacefully," his best friend said in his message. Were healing and peace for him possible only in his dying? Not long ago, he had been filled with fear as he anticipated death. Had he come to know a peace that before had been beyond all of his understanding? Had God acted in his heart in ways none of his friends could have imagined? I live in hope that he did come to know himself as a beloved child of God.

As the crowd gathered for William's memorial service, I watched in wonder. Two pastors moved to the front of the sanctuary. One served the church in which we were gathered. It was a church where William had found a home many years ago when he felt unwelcome in other congregations. The other pastor served the mainline suburban congregation where William had played the organ. I know both pastors. Because of their different perspectives regarding the Christian faith, many would have found it unimaginable that they would stand together, in this church, sharing the leadership of worship. Yet, both loved William. Both proclaimed God's unfailing grace. This night, they belonged together.

> How do you see healing in Margaret Kim Peterson's story of her husband? Spend a few moments remembering your own experiences and those of persons close to you. Have there been times when "healing" came in ways that were unexpected? Do you know of those who would describe experiences in the way Margaret Kim Peterson did: "How could we have asked for it, *when we couldn't even imagine it?*" Talk about the experiences you remember.

The pastors proclaimed their words of affection for William and witnessed to the ways in which William gave and received love and grace.

21

Then others spoke. "I have never known anyone who had so many devoted friends," one said. Heads nodded. Laughter filled the sanctuary as we listened to stories about William's idiosyncrasies and sometimes less than cooperative demeanor. The church organist closed the service with one of the songs William loved to play. We smiled, but we knew it was not as William would have played it; the floor did not shake.

Four older women from the suburban congregation walked quietly from their pew, nodding sadly, two wiping tears from their cheeks. William's best friend was distributing invitations for the after-service celebration. Together we all stood in the foyer, telling more William stories and remembering.

In those moments, I had a sense that William would have been looking around at this crowd, shaking his head in wonder, and saying: "I never knew so many of you cared." And then he would have exclaimed, with the frustration he sometimes exhibited at such times, "Why did it take my dying to bring you all together in church?"

I do not know how William's living and dying will change our lives. I believed that evening that God had been working within both William and his friends in those last weeks and days, when his hospital room was continually full, to assure him that he was indeed loved. I also felt as if God was working within all of us, reminding us not to delay in expressing our love for those around us.

I wonder if God was acting in other ways, far beyond all we knew how to ask or imagine, to bring a glimpse of what it might be for sisters and brothers in Christ to live together— no longer alienated by our differences and divisions. Was it an intimation of God's reign? People living together, loving together, praying and praising together—not ignoring their differences, but celebrating our unity in grace.

In the midst of brokenness in the church and in the community, might there have been among us a beginning of the healing?

What of the ache in my own heart that lives beside every joy? Several years into my grief and loss, I began

> How do you see healing in the story of William's funeral? How do you think divine healing occurs when people come together to celebrate a person's life and to grieve their loss through death? What experiences do you know about in which a church community has experienced divine healing for brokenness or for conflict? In what ways, if any, was worship a factor in the healing?

to write letters—letters that, years and many tears later, formed a book.[6] I am not sure what I anticipated as I began to write, what I wanted Jesus to do for me. Acquaintances assumed the writing was "cathartic" and "helped with closure"; for, as Irish journalist Nuala O'Faolain says, "There is an idea current in the prevailing culture that writing about something that pains you heals the pain."[7] It did not for her, nor for me.

O'Faolain writes further and puts words to my experience:

> I found out when I was a little girl that if you're crying uncontrollably and want to stop, the thing is to do something useful with your tears—water a plant, say.[8]

Writing seemed to be useful. I knew how to do it. Maybe something would grow.

Shortly after reading my book, a friend who had been shattered by the death of her only child, sent me a message. One phrase has lived with me each day since:

You give me hope.

After that, little else about the book mattered. It did not matter how many books were sold or what a review said. I feared my friend's spirit was irretrievably broken. To discover that God was working within her now in this way was far beyond all I would have known to ask.

While my friend's response was a sufficient blessing, I did hear from many whose pain was touched by mine. It was not closure or resolution that came in the writing. My experience feels like that of O'Faolain: "It was the warmth the book met that had made me strong."[9]

> How do you see divine healing in Vogel's way of dealing with her grief over the loss of her son? Look at the definitions of healing that you made at the beginning of the session. How have the stories informed your earlier definitions? How do you define *divine healing* after hearing and conversing with these stories? What else that may not have been suggested in the stories would you add to your list of definitions? Create a group definition of *divine healing*.

23

"What do you want me to do for you?"

How could we have asked for it,

"I came that they may have life, and have it abundantly."

When we couldn't even imagine it?

What is healing?

We have begun to walk paths toward a wider and deeper consciousness. Together we will seek other paths in the pages that follow. But we will not ever know all that the mystery of God has for us.
God in Jesus Christ wants for you
life abundant and full,
more and better than you could ever dream.

Closing
Sing two or three times: "Come and Fill Our Hearts." Then join in these prayers:

O God, . . . take the chaos and confusion and disorder of our minds and spirits and hold them so completely in Thy grasp that the impure thing will become pure, . . . and the crass and hard thing will be gentled by Thy spirit. . . . Amen. [10]
—Howard Thurman

Lord, never let me sleep until
I have stretched my hands over my village
and invoked your blessing on it. . . . Amen.[11]
—Michel Bouttier

Notes

1. "Come and Fill Our Hearts" can be found in *The Faith We Sing* (Nashville: Abingdon Press, 2000), number 2157.
2. Samuel H. Miller, *Prayers for Daily Use* (New York: Harper & Brothers Publishers, 1957), page 90. Your group may prefer to pray this adaptation:

Center us down, O God, until in our deepest soul we kneel, quietly, waitfully, reverently. Deliver us from the world for these brief moments, so that we may meet [you] undistractedly, and confirm the bond that binds us to [you]. Then in [your] presence help us to reorder our minds and hearts, bringing before[you] one by one our loved ones, our hopes and fears, our great joys and our ill-admitted sins, until we see with [your] eyes and love with [your] grace.

3. Eugene Peterson's paraphrase of the Bible is now complete. Parts of Peterson's language are stark, and too idiomatic for some. It seldom fails, however, to break open fresh dimensions of meaning for the reader.

4. Margaret Kim Peterson, *Sing Me to Heaven* (Grand Rapids, MI: Brazos Press, 2003), page 134. This book is a useful resource for those who want to read further about how Peterson understands healing as distinguished from curing.

5. *Sing Me to Heaven,* page 135.

6. Susan Sonnenday Vogel, *And Then Mark Died: Letters of Grief, Love, and Faith* (Nashville: Abingdon Press, 2003).

7. Nuala O' Faolain, *Almost There: The Onward Journey of a Dublin Woman* (New York: Riverhead Books, 2003), page 36.

8. *Almost There,* pages 36–37.

9. Nuala O'Faolain, *Are You Somebody? The Accidental Memoir of a Dublin Woman* (New York: Henry Holt and Company, 1996), page 214.

10. Howard Thurman, *The Centering Moment* (New York: Harper & Row, 1969), page 112. Howard Thurman was a pastor and teacher whom a colleague called "the premier African American spiritual genius of the 20th century."

11. Michel Bouttier, *Prayers for My Village* (Nashville: Upper Room Books, 1994), page 58.

CHAPTER 2
"DO YOU WANT
TO BE MADE WELL?"

Is divine healing always worth the price?

Focus: This chapter explores the connections between the divine and human roles in healing—ourselves, our loved ones, our churches, and our communities.

Gathering
Sing together two or three times "Come and Fill Our Hearts."[1]
Then join together in prayer:

Center us down, O God, until in our deepest soul we kneel, quietly, waitfully, reverently. Deliver us from the world for these brief moments, so that we may meet thee undistractedly, and confirm the bond that binds us to thee. Then in thy presence help us to reorder our minds and hearts, bringing before thee one by one our loved ones, our hopes and fears, our great joys and our ill-admitted sins, until we see with thine eyes and love with thy grace.[2]

After a few moments of silence, lift concerns for healing that are on your hearts. All respond in prayer: *We bring this care before you.*
Close with these words: *Help us to reorder our minds and hearts, until we see with your eyes and love with your grace. Amen.*

A Peculiar Question

John 5 tells a story about a healing that points to the tension between God's healing and the human response, in the individual and in the community, to God's healing activity. The story focuses on a conversation between Jesus and a man who had been ill for thirty-eight years and who sought the healing properties of a pool called Bethesda.[3] The King James version of this story includes a verse that says that in certain seasons an angel "troubled" the water, and the first person to enter the water after the "troubling" would be healed. Jesus asks the man a peculiar question:

"Do you want to be made well?" (John 5:6)

Why would Jesus ask such a question? Is the answer not obvious? What can possibly be happening here? For how long has this man been waiting by the pool? The Scripture reports that Jesus knew he had been lying beside the pool a long time. Why else would the man be there if he did not want to be made well?

> Read John 5:2-9. Why do you think Jesus asks the man, "Do you want to be made well?"

A Human Response

What is the man's response? His answer is almost as peculiar as Jesus' question. He doesn't say, "Yes." He tells Jesus why he has not been healed. "Sir, I have no one to put me into the pool when the water is stirred up; and while I am making my way, someone else steps down ahead of me." How would we answer? Could we have answered Jesus' question with a simple "Yes"? Do we want to be healed?

One of my pastors used a phrase I often bring now to Scripture. "I like to use my sanctified imagination," he said. Then he would take us into the story as we might have experienced it had we been there. This is sometimes a part of *lectio divina,* a practice of *holy reading* of Scripture. In this kind of reading, the goal is to listen to ways God speaks to us in the biblical text and to discern how the text might inform our lives. Use your sanctified imagination as you consider what the man beside the pool might have thought:

Of course I want to be healed. Why else would I be camped out at

27

> Read aloud the question "Do you want to be made well?" Imagine Jesus is speaking to you. In what way do you need to be made well? Is something keeping you from being made well? If so, what is it? Walk into this story with your sanctified imagination and with your need for divine healing. Hear the question for yourself. What will you answer?
>
> After living for some moments in your sanctified imagination, make notes for yourself about your answer(s).

this pool for a long time? But surely that is not what Jesus is asking. He must mean, "Now why is it you have not managed to be made well before?" I do know how to answer that question. Others have asked me that. I know the answer well. I can explain carefully, and in detail, why it has been impossible to be made well. I could not get to the pool. No one would help me.

But Jesus does not listen to my answer. He ignores what I have to say. He does not even agree with my prescription for healing; he will not put me in the waters of the pool. Jesus gives me new instructions. He assumes I am already well. He tells me to stand up, take my mat, and walk.

"Do you want to be made well?"

Of course the man wants to be healed. But if the desire to be healed is that clear, why would Jesus ask? And, if he asks the man by the pool, is he also asking each of us—now? What will *we* answer?

"Do you want to be made well?"

As I lived with this story for several weeks, I grew aware that I had not *listened* to the question before. I had not ever imagined how I would answer. My head *knew* the right answer. Of course, the man wanted to be healed. And, of course, I want to be made well. But what does my heart feel—and say—when faced with that question? What have I felt and said as I have been asked that question through the years? And what is my role, my *human* role in divine healing?

Do you want rest? Do you want to be made well?
I am so weary. I feel overwhelmed at times. I talk of the importance of sabbath, and it is just so hard to keep going. Let me explain. This time of year is full of responsibilities. I could not possibly think of

taking any time away. I do not have anyone to do just what I do; there is no one who can help.

Do you want physical health and vitality? Do you want to be made well?

And I know I need to exercise more. I read about how important it is. I have friends who have joined a new women's health club with a pool.

What plan do you have? Do you want to be made well?

You don't understand. I have never been very good at planning. I always do better if I wait until I feel ready. I also do not do well alone, and there is no one I know who wants to go to the pool with me.

Do we want to be made well? Not only do we want to, we know we must—if we want to live. But it really is hard to get to that pool, and often we feel that we cannot do it alone. We feel that no one will help us.

> How would you respond to the questions? What are the healing pools you desire to enter, know you must enter, yet feel you have no help to enter?

Change and Transitions

I heard a wise woman say once, "No one likes change. We all just want things to get better." I want to be better. I want everything around me to be better. I want to be made well, and I want those around me and the situations in which I work and pray and play to be made well. Yes, I believe we all want to be made well. But few of us want change. It is too hard.

That is not quite it either, William Bridges teaches us. It is not *change* that is the problem, Bridges suggests. It is *transition* that is too hard.

Bridges says, *"Change* is a situational shift."[5] We lose a job or a new president comes to the institution. We

> **For Further Information**
> William Bridges has written a series of books on the description, significance, and implications of transition for our personal and professional lives and for the lives of our institutions and organizations. Among these are: *Transitions, Managing Transitions,* and *The Way of Transition.* Some may want to explore this area more extensively.[4]

have a new baby, or a son dies. A congregation gets a new pastor, or the church burns.

> *Transition,* on the other hand, is the process of letting go of the way things used to be [before the change] and then taking hold of the way they subsequently become. In between the letting go and the taking hold again, there is a chaotic but potentially creative "neutral zone" when things aren't the old way, but aren't really a new way yet either.[6]

Transition, Bridges says, is all three of these phases: the letting go and ending, the neutral zone in-between, and the beginning anew.

I have found Bridges's work to be a missing piece in my understandings of change, and I am grateful for the way he has put words to what I have lived. His insights have been informing as I continue the struggle to understand what healing means and how it happens—or does not happen.

Is It My Fault If I Am Not Healed?

We can often see truth in humor and the twisting of truth into hyperbole. As I have been studying questions related to healing and change, I keep hearing in my mind one of those silly light bulb jokes. How many psychologists does it take to change a light bulb? Only one, but the light bulb must want to be changed.

A truth—carried in inappropriate directions or to extremes—can become a destructive un-truth. So it is with healing and wanting to be made well. We can learn much by looking at the painful challenges of change and transition and what happens to us when we are asked if we want to become something different. In some situations, *wanting to be made well* is a critical element in healing. Learning to let go of a state of brokenness and taking hold of new life is seldom simple, and we have to want to do that hard work.

> Have you felt you are being "blamed" for your suffering? Have there been times you have held others responsible for their illness? Do you think holding others responsible for their illness is ever legitimate? Why or why not?

These understandings have sometimes been used as "weapons" and, rather than becoming aids to healing, have served to increase pain and guilt. Then we not only are sick or grieving or alienated from family or

30

out of work, we are also guilty and overburdened because we have not managed to overcome whatever is wrong. We must not have wanted healing in the right way.

Leo, a character in a novel by Ursula Hegi, has just returned from visiting his native Germany and is explaining to Helene:

"They don't understand that when you come back, you're not the same. And neither are they. It's like that with grieving . . . you enter a foreign country. And sometimes you don't come back."

Helene asks, "Unless you want to?" Leo responds:

"Oh, but wanting to come back is just a small part of it, Helene."[7]

There are times when "wanting to come back" or "wanting to be healed" is just a small part of it. We may not have the strength or the tools for the healing that we need.

Did I Have Enough Faith?

In the life of the church, a variation on "blaming" ourselves and others for lack of healing happens when we see "faith" as a requirement for God's healing in our lives and fear we do not have "enough." If we are not healed, or if our loved one dies, was it because our faith was lacking?

I recall the sense of relief a student expressed when she discovered that "faith" is linked with healing in only a few of the Jesus healing narratives. In fact, faith sometimes follows the healing (John 4:46-54). The student could not wait to take her "good news" to the parishioner who repeatedly berated herself for her illness and lamented, "Jesus says if I had faith enough, I would be well."

> Consider these Scriptures from the Gospels that link faith and healing: Mark 5:25-34, Mark 10:46-52, and Matthew 15:21-28. Contrast these Scriptures with Luke 5:17-26 and Matthew 9:2-8. What seems to be the purpose of the healing in these Scriptures? What connections do you see between healing and faith? How do these Scriptures inform your understanding of divine healing?

The Neutral Zone

Although letting go of the old and taking hold of a new way are critical tasks, it is often the "in-between," what Bridges calls "the neutral zone," that is the greatest challenge. *Neutral zone* hardly seems an adequate description.[8]

31

Bridges borrows the term "neutral zone" from the work of the Dutch anthropologist Arnold van Gennep, the author of *Rites of Passage.* It was van Gennep who first came to see the commonalities among tribal rituals that acted out a letting go of one life stage and a moving into another. These rituals parallel what Bridges means by "transitions." We often see these rituals as "primitive," but they were critical elements in keeping the social order intact.[9]

As I look back at the transitions in my own life, I know those in-between times as both chaotic and creative, yes, but also filled with such an intensity of pain and confusion that *neutral* feels like a strange choice of words. Long ago, as I was beginning to question what the church and society around me said a *woman* must be, I read with a frightening sense of recognition words of theologian Mary Daly:

Finally, there is the anxiety of meaninglessness, which can be overwhelming at times when the old simple meanings, role definitions, and life expectations have been rooted out and rejected openly and one emerges into a world without models.[10]

I can still remember the feeling—it comes back as I write—an ache in my chest and tears ready to pour forth. Her words captured my own sense of chaos and lost-ness in those days. A young woman named Dorie Ellzey expressed the feeling in a song as she imagined each of us like Lillith,[11] coming out of the garden. "Somebody help me," she cries. She is out of the garden. She is on her own, and she feels lost. And then the image: "I'm in the water, but the bathtub is gone."[12]

We could laugh sometimes as we sang together; but then there was the nod of recognition, the ache, the tears. We were in between. We knew we could not go back, the song continued. We also had no idea what was ahead. We could only "stumble along." Nothing felt *neutral* then. Years later, Joan Chittister said it anew as she reflected upon a verse from Ecclesiastes—"A Time for Weeping."

Weeping signals change as well as loss. . . . When the present ceases to fit and the future has yet no definition, tears oil the way between the two. Tears lead us from loss to change.[13]

Samuel Miller speaks of the time when "the surface of life is ripped off . . . . [and] the soul . . . must handle mystery with its naked hands."[14]

If any of these words or images touch a place in your heart, you know transition. *Transition* or *neutral zone* can sound analytical and sterile. But those who have been there, or are living there now, know the bruised flesh and aching heart and confusion and pain that go with this not-knowing place of wilderness and mystery and chaos.

> What other examples can you name in which cultural change or transition was needed in order for people to find healing and wholeness? What connections do you make between these examples and divine healing of groups, churches, or communities?

Reactive and Developmental Transition

Bridges writes that these transitions are of at least two kinds: A *reactive* transition is one set off "by a specific, external change" and "represents the way that people deal with or get through the change." A *developmental* transition is produced by an "unfolding of . . . who we are." It is "any profound shift to a new way of experiencing the world."[15]

In my own life, the death of my son led to a reactive transition; a tragic event changed me into a mourning mother, and I had to live into and through years of transition. The earlier experience when I was "in the water and the bathtub was gone" was a developmental one. I found myself experiencing the world in a radically different way, and out of that wilderness time had to come changes in how I lived my life. Living into life without my son? Becoming a woman different from what I had been taught by every image around me for thirty years? How can I ever do that?

Resistance to Transition

William Bridges helps us understand the ways in which transition can be daunting. He writes that our resistance to transition can take several forms—or a combination of them.[16] We may resist letting go of what has been and letting go of the "me," or that part of us that has that lived what has been. Or we may become discouraged about our time in the in-between space. We can only tread water for so long. We run out of tears. We cannot stand the not-knowing or meaninglessness, the sense of wilderness and wandering. We cannot live any longer with such ambiguity, not being able to stand on firm ground. Or we may have a difficult

33

time grasping a new beginning. Perhaps we feel it will be a betrayal of the past. We cannot imagine our lives in a different way.

To say we resist transition may be misleading if we think resistance means a cognitive, rational decision not to let go or not to enter into a new beginning. The tasks of any of these phases can become overwhelming. It takes time to live into them. How can we possibly let go? It is not some *thing* we are leaving. It is the "me" that we have shaped—carefully and, perhaps, sometimes carelessly—up to this point. Samuel Miller has written graphically, about that *me*:

> Here in us, in these capacious hearts of ours, we carry strange peremptory devils who came to us in other days, came quietly and slowly at first with much courtesy and bright wit and enticing manners, but now that they are no longer casual guests but established members of our soul they act as masters and hold us to their will. Here in these hearts are the compromises we lightly made with the world, harmless and seemingly necessary ones at the time, but full of interminable and growing consequences. All of these we would like to repudiate, but habit being what it is, we will continue to the end of time, justifying ourselves with high-sounding but hollow phrases.[17]

In our hearts are "entanglements," all that other people "say and think we are." It is as if these are "stakes . . . to which we have been tied—and who is there who will act out of character, do what is unexpected . . ., dare to defy self-consistency . . .?"[18]

Nuala O'Faolain describes the way families do not allow members "to experiment with themselves":

> The penalty for being loyally accepted for the whole of your life is that you must stay what you always were. . . . Reinvention is not possible.[19]

Let go? Is anyone surprised that we should have trouble letting go? We are likely to say something like, "This is all I know. This is who I am. Let go of what? of myself? the only self I know? It may not be a very healthy self, but it is the only one I have." This self is the one who has, figuratively speaking, been sitting by the pool for a long time, the self who has been ill for thirty-eight years. It is difficult to imagine any other self we might become.

Do you want to be made well?

Again, we listen to what the man beside the pool might have been thinking:

How do I know? I do not know anything but this life.

I waited and waited to get into the water, but no one would help me. Now this man comes, whose name I do not know. He tells me to pick up my mat and walk. It was not the water I needed for healing after all. He says I am made well.

Who am I now? I am not the man waiting by the pool. That is who I have been all those years. Who am I now?

I am not sure. I am afraid.

Moving Through Healing to Wholeness

Whatever else healing is, it means change and transition. Healing has to do with moving from one state, which we call illness or alienation or brokenness, to another way of being, which we call wholeness, reconciliation, abundant life. Something happens. Something is different. It may not be different in the way I anticipated, but something is different.

Bridges describes *change* as what happens on the outside. It is *transition* that happens on the inside—the inside of individuals, organizations, nations, churches. It is the letting go, the wandering in-between, the taking hold of something new. Could it be that healing is often more about transition (in this sense) than change? Is it in transition that God works with me so I can "let go of" brokenness and "take hold of" wholeness?

It may be that we discover our need for healing as we find ourselves in that in-between place—thrown there by a life-changing event or unfolded into a new way of experiencing the world. We discover our need when we wake up and there we are in the water and the bathtub is gone.

The extent of pain or confusion or disorientation we know in the in-between place may give us a window into how hard healing will be and what we will need in order to find our way through that wilderness. Bridges names what most of us already know: it is in that wilderness place that we "most readily encounter The Sacred."[20] To return to the stark image of Samuel Miller: "the surface of life is ripped off . . . . [and] the

35

soul . . . must handle mystery with its naked hands."[21] The soul moves to a place it could not know before.

It is in the wilderness of chaos and pain that God meets us. And in meeting God, we learn what we must learn to move on. God offers manna, enough for every day. God sends companions with whom to wrestle and from whom, finally, to receive a blessing. God turns us into the storm and stays with us so we will live. But the wilderness is treacherous. We may give up and go back to Egypt.

Do we want to be made well? Do we want to live life in all its abundance? Indeed. And yet, is it worth the price? Is it worth the risk?

My friend Fran tells of a fire in the fraternity house where her son lived. His burns were extensive and severe. She flew across the country to the hospital to keep vigil beside him. As he began to heal, the nurses had to scrub away the old skin so that new healthy skin would grow. Fran listened to her son's cries of pain, and her heart was breaking. Then the doctors said she could bring him home—if she would do the scrubbing.

Do we want to be made well? Do we want others around us to be made well? What are we willing to do? What will we need for God to do for us in the wilderness? Yes, we want to be made well. And, yet, we simply cannot get to the pool. No one will help us. And what if we get to the pool, and that is not the answer? Could it be that getting to the pool may not be the only option?

Pick Up Your Mat and Walk

Now we have picked up our mats and left the pool. We are in that in-between place where we must live for a time and discover the ways God is providing companions and nourishment—until we can discern that to which God's healing is leading us. Questions and new ways to see healing lead into more questions and few certainties. That is what it must mean to move to "a deeper and wider consciousness . . . to which we are carried . . . by virtue of having wrestled"[22] with these questions. It helps me to recall part of a confession from Howard Thurman:

> We are mindful of our weaknesses, the things which we have tried to overcome for so long a time, and yet which dog our footsteps and never seem to lose the scent of our trail. . . .[23]

Closing
Sing two or three times in closing: "Come and Fill Our Hearts." Then join in these prayers:

O God, . . . take the chaos and confusion and disorder of our minds and spirits and hold them so completely in Thy grasp that the impure thing will become pure, . . . and the crass and hard thing will be gentled by Thy spirit. . . . Amen.[24]
—Howard Thurman

And, Lord, never let me sleep
until I have stretched my hands over my village
and invoked your blessings on it. . . . Amen.[25]
—Michel Bouttier

Notes

1. "Come and Fill Our Hearts" can be found in *The Faith We Sing* (Nashville: Abingdon Press, 2000), number 2157.
2. Samuel H. Miller, *Prayers for Daily Use* (New York: Harper & Brothers Publishers, 1957), page 90. Your group may prefer to pray this adaptation: *Center us down, O God, until in our deepest soul we kneel, quietly, waitfully, reverently. Deliver us from the world for these brief moments, so that we may meet [you] undistractedly, and confirm the bond that binds us to [you]. Then in [your] presence help us to reorder our minds and hearts, bringing before[you] one by one our loved ones, our hopes and fears, our great joys and our ill-admitted sins, until we see with [your] eyes and love with [your] grace.*
3. This pool is named Beth-zatha in the NRSV and Bethsaida and Bethesda in other translations of the Bible.
4. William Bridges, *Managing Transitions: Making the Most of Change* (Cambridge, Mass.: Perseus Publishing, 1991). *Transitions: Making Sense of Life's Changes* (Reading, MA: Pearson Addison Wesley, 1980). *The Way of Transition: Embracing Life's Most Difficult Moments* (Cambridge, Mass.: Perseus Publishing, 2000).
5. *The Way of Transition*, page 2.
6. *The Way of Transition*, page 2.
7. Ursula Hegi, *The Vision of Emma Blau* (New York: Simon & Schuster, 2000), page 162.
8. *The Way of Transition*, pages 5–6.
9. *The Way of Transition*, pages 7–8.
10. Mary Daly, *Beyond God the Father* (Boston: Beacon Press, 1974), page 24.

11. There is an extra-canonical story that Lillith was the first woman in the primordial garden. She was banished from the garden to wander on her own.

12. "Out of the Garden," copyright 1974, Doris J. Ellzey. Used by permission from the published music & songbook collection *No Way to Stop This Miracle,* copyright 1985 by Dorie Ellzey Blesoff. *www.dorieLZblesoff.com.*

13. Joan Chittister, *There is a Season* (Maryknoll, NY: Orbis Books, 1995), pages 90–91.

14. Samuel H. Miller, *The Life of The Church* (New York: Harper & Brothers, 1953), page 32.

15. *The Way of Transition*, pages 4–5.

16. *The Way of Transition,* pages 3–4.

17. Samuel H. Miller, *The Life of the Soul* (New York: Harper & Row, 1951), page 130.

18. *The Life of the Soul,* page 131.

19. Nuala O' Faolain, *Almost There: The Onward Journey of a Dublin Woman* (New York: Riverhead Books, 2003), page 180.

20. *The Way of Transition*, page 40.

21. *The Life of The Church*, page 32.

22. Rollo May, *Love and Will* (New York: W. W. Norton and Company, 1969), pages 170–71.

23. Howard Thurman, *The Centering Moment* (New York: Harper & Row, 1969), page 86.

24. *The Centering Moment*, page 112.

25. Michel Bouttier, *Prayers for My Village* (Nashville: Upper Room Books, 1994), page 58.

CHAPTER 3
"NOW YOU ARE
THE BODY OF CHRIST"

How do we need one another for healing?

Focus: This chapter explores God's divine healing as it works through relationship with others. In both personal healing and in the healing of families, churches, communities, and other groups, we need one another.

Gathering

Sing together two or three times "Come and Fill Our Hearts."[1] Then join together in prayer:

Center us down, O God, until in our deepest soul we kneel, quietly, waitfully, reverently. Deliver us from the world for these brief moments, so that we may meet thee undistractedly, and confirm the bond that binds us to thee. Then in thy presence help us to reorder our minds and hearts, bringing before thee one by one our loved ones, our hopes and fears, our great joys and our ill-admitted sins, until we see with thine eyes and love with thy grace. [2]

After a few moments of silence, lift concerns for healing that are on your hearts. All respond in prayer: *We bring this care before you.*

Close with these words: *Help us to reorder our minds and hearts, until we see with your eyes and love with your grace. Amen.*

Self-Sufficiency

A creative, brilliant, and grieving young woman has been on my heart. She and her mother are dear to me. Imagine her name is Meredith, and her mother is Elisabeth. Meredith was about to complete college when her father, from whom she had been estranged, became ill and soon died. Meredith arrived at the hospital in time to spend some of her father's last moments with him.

Meredith stayed at home for a time, reluctant to return to school and the work awaiting completion. When she did return, she was not able to re-engage her work and was seldom in touch with her family. Elisabeth waited. One morning she sent word that she had heard from Meredith:

> I got a short email last night. She told me not to worry, that she was ok and working 60 hours a week. She said she was learning to become self-sufficient but it was very tiring.

She was learning to become self-sufficient, but it was very tiring.

Those words stung my heart. I sent a message to Elisabeth saying we were thankful and relieved, and then I wrote:

> One has to wonder, though, where the myth comes from that any of us has to be or can be self-sufficient. I fear it is a part of the culture that is at odds with what is one of the better parts of the Christian tradition. I often quote to my students a paraphrase of what one of the saints of the church said, "God could have made us perfect, but God chose not to so that we would need one another." *We* know that. Maybe, in time, it will be all right for Meredith to come to know that. Until then, we will wait and watch and pray.

Many years before, in a quite different cultural context, Richard Wright wrote in *Black Boy* of his own growing up and his paradoxical relationship to the young men around him:

What is your response to Meredith's desire to be "self-sufficient"? What connections do you see between her need to become more self-sufficient and the loss of her father? How do you see divine healing or the need for divine healing in her situation? How do you understand self-sufficiency? What are its strengths? its weaknesses?

[W]e pretended callousness toward the injunctions of our parents; and we strove to convince one another that our decisions stemmed from ourselves and ourselves alone. Yet we frantically concealed how dependent we were upon one another.[3]

> Consider examples around you that lift up "self-sufficiency" as a positive value. Do you find that message in the church? If so, in what ways?

Self-sufficient? A need to appear *independent?* What can that possibly mean? From where do we receive that message?

Catherine of Siena, one of our foremothers in the faith, reported what she heard God saying in one of her visions (the words I paraphrase as "God could have made us perfect . . ."):

> I could well have supplied each of you with all your needs, both spiritual and material. But I wanted to make you dependent on one another so that each of you would be my minister, dispensing the graces and gifts you have received from me.[4]

And in different images, another of our foremothers, Julian of Norwich, wrote of our need to look to the "Holy Church" in our times of suffering:

> For one single person may often be broken, as it seems to him, but the entire body of Holy Church was never broken, nor ever will be without end.[5]

Julian calls the suffering one to be "united" to our "mother Holy Church, who is Christ Jesus." Then, "The sweet gracious hands of our Mother are ready and diligent about us; . . ."[6]

Both of these women lived in the Scriptures. They may have been prepared to hear these words and see these visions through their familiarity with the letter of Paul to his sisters and brothers in Corinth.

> Read 1 Corinthians 12:12-31. What might Paul say to my young friend Meredith and to her mother? to the teenaged Richard Wright and his friends?

A Healing Presence of Family and Friends

Near the close of Chapter 2, I wrote of my friend Fran and the agonizing treatment she had to provide for her son's burns so that he would know healing. Fifty years ago, the treatment was different.

41

Early one October morning, I stood at the stove in the kitchen, perched on a kitchen chair. I was too short to reach the top of the old percolator in which I was making coffee to surprise Mommy and Daddy. Then something was wrong. Steam was pushing up around the edges of the pot. I tried to push the top down, but suddenly it exploded. Boiling water flew everywhere.

Daddy, who *never* hurried, rushed down the steps. Mommy followed. They tore off the soaked nightgown and wrapped a blanket around me. Dr. Schwartz soon was at the door and immediately started to work. Slowly, with painstaking care, he picked the coffee grounds off my skin, applied soothing ointment, and then wrapped me in gauze bandages, mummy-like, in which I lived for several weeks. "You can keep her at home," he said, "as long as she gets plenty of liquid and you watch for signs of shock. Someone needs to be close by all the time."

I have many memories surrounding these events when I was nine years old; it was the first time I had been seriously hurt or ill. There are a few "bad" memories—the fear that something terrible was happening and the initial pain of the burns. But, strangely, my foremost memories of that time are warm and good ones: memories of abundant care and love, tender acts of mercy and healing—coming from many different ones upon whom I had to depend, who, for the moment, were not broken as I was broken.

Granddaddy soon arrived, and as he was sitting beside me, I told him I felt sick. The next image I remember is my very large grandfather, in his three-piece suit, hurrying into the room and reaching out to me with a very small saucepan. I laugh now at the incongruity of the image, but it was symbolic of much that happened in those days and weeks. Everyone around me reached out in a distinctive way. Each one became part of my healing. Daddy came home each afternoon to watch the World Series with me, patiently answering my string of questions about the Giants and the Yankees. Mother created a Coke "slush," before others had imagined such a thing. What a luxury to have Coke at home. My handsome teenaged neighbor gave me more attention than I had dared hope: "Suz—don't you know you are supposed to *drink* coffee, not take a bath in it!" My classmates brought my schoolwork home and returned my completed assignments to my teacher. Piles of cards covered the dining room table. "We are praying for you," said the notes and telephone calls.

I was fortunate. Healing happened. The shock and emotional trauma that the doctor had feared did not come to be. A whole village surrounded me, and I knew healing as each brought a special gift that another could not offer. Healing happened because of what each one *did* and in the ways these special people were *with* me. It is the details about how they were *with* me that I still treasure and can recount after fifty-two years. They were "dispensing the gifts and graces" they had received from God. I could not have said it then, but today I witness to my conviction that I knew God's healing in the workings of that constellation of family and friends. I was enfolded and loved into healing by my community in ways beyond what I might ever have dreamed. The healing was more than new skin covering my body. I was in relationship with my community, and each one in it, in a new way. I was connected with Daddy—bonded by the love of baseball I had discovered, but more than that. He had taken time away from work for *me*, and I trusted his love in a way I had not known before. It must have affected our whole family; for our bread-winning father, in 1951, there was something more important than work. When I returned to school, my peers saw me as one who needed help; I was no longer the "smart one" who intimidated them.

> What experiences of the healing presence of family and friends do you have? How do you think divine healing occurs in such situations?

Interdependency

In recent years, I have read the work of Margaret Wheatley and was carried back in time to that village that surrounded me. "We are utterly intertwined," Wheatley writes. "Everything is the result of interdependencies."[7] "[T]he meaning of who we are changes through our communion with [others]."[8]

It is dangerous, a friend reminds me, to say "all" and "everything." Yet, Wheatley points to truth that fills our Scriptures and traditions and experience. I do not see God working apart from the way Catherine of Siena described. We need one another. We need our sisters and brothers

> **For More Information**
> Margaret Wheatley invites us to learn from the way all life organizes itself. She suggests that we may discover new models for our ways of being with one another by looking, for example, at "the new science" of chaos theory and quantum physics. See especially *Leadership and the New Science* and *A Simpler Way.*[7]

43

> Form three teams. Ask each team to read and discuss one of the following Scriptures and discuss the following questions: 1 Kings 17:8-24; Mark 2:1-12; and Mark 14:3-9. How does divine healing occur? What does the Scripture suggest about self-sufficiency? about interdependency? Through whom has God brought healing in your life? How have you seen God work through your own gifts and graces to offer healing for another?

to whom God has given the gifts and graces to make us whole.

It Takes a Village

As I look back at Meredith's message in light of my own experience and the wisdom I read in Scripture and tradition, my heart still aches.

She said she was learning to become self-sufficient, but it was very tiring.

"It was very tiring." Finally, I fear, it will be exhausting, completely exhausting. It takes a village, a community, the entire body, to care for one of its parts. In ordinary times, we only live because God sustains us through the gifts that come to us through other people, moment by moment. But it is in times of tragedy or injury or dis-ease that I am clear that I will die without the care of the whole body. As I wrote about my healing following Mark's death, I said to those who had stayed close to me through those hardest times:

> You have saved my life. You, who have been there rightly, saved my life.
> You are legion. It requires a legion to save the life of a grieving mother.
> My grieving is too much for one of you. Together, you saved my life.[9]

An assuring sense of recognition touched me when I read similar words my friend Pam wrote after her young husband had died suddenly: She entitled one section of her reflections, "It Takes a Village to Raise a Widow":

> We were standing because of the countless praying hands that surrounded our three bodies, willing us to defy the gravitational pull downward.
> Our ability to stand was the foreshadowing of another permanent landscape change: we were not alone. Gathered silently on either side of my children and me was a continuous stream of faithful witnesses. Tears in their eyes, they had come to hold our hands. They came bearing donuts, meatballs, lawnmowers and flowers.[10]

Healing as Restored Relationship

As my heart aches with Elisabeth and Meredith, another creative and confusingly brilliant young person has been on my heart as well. His name is Philip, and his mother is Jenee. Jenee has an extraordinary mind and was a superior seminary student many years ago. I wrote to her asking her perspectives on healing; for Jenee is a perpetual student, and Philip has led her to a concern for healing that is more than theoretical. Philip lives with a severe and unusual form of autism. He is essentially nonverbal but has a remarkable array of other skills. He is partial to machines—especially computers and electronics; he wires circuits, programs robotics, and helps his teachers with computer problems.[11]

As Jenee has studied Scripture and lived with the challenges of Philip's condition, she has helped me understand healing in the Gospels in the context of relationship—especially relationship within community. If one was not well, in body or spirit, then that often meant separation from the community: the leper and the woman with the flow of blood were unclean; another woman was "filled with demons." Healing often meant the restoring of relationship between the one who was "ill" and the wider community in a way that changed both. So, while the person might not be "cured," in the way they or others wanted or expected, the person was put into right relationship with the people in the community. Something happened to *both* parties—and what was "wrong" with the person (in a social sense) was no longer wrong. The "healed" person became a "healed healer"—healing not only others who have a dis-ease in the terms of the community but also those who believe themselves to be "well." I thought about myself at age nine. I saw myself, and my father, and my classmates, and our constellation of community; healing happened among us, in our relationships.

Jenee reflects on how significant this understanding has been for her in relation to her son. He walks into a room and, as she says, "doesn't get it" in the way "everyone else gets it." As the community faces who they are with Philip, and comes to understand that he is every bit a child of God like the rest of us, then something new happens.

> In some way, as folks accept him as "completely human," that is a healing thing for them—spiritually at the very least, and in the ways that physical healing and health are connected with spiritual healing and health. He has a way

45

of stripping things down to their essentials, for all who bother to relate to him.

Whatever conditions and definitions we place on "being human" fly right out the window when one has much contact with my son. Whatever "wholeness" or "salvation" is about, God works it out in relation to people like *him*—people who ... just plain *cannot* do the things we continue to insist folks "have to" do in order to receive the grace of God. And in all of that, I think, is a kind of surgical healing—repentance and forgiveness, maybe.... I've seen it happen with many folks, and it happens over and over again for me. My son is a healer.[12]

God works in and through relationships so we may bring healing to one another. As Margaret Wheatley has written,

> Relationships change us, reveal us, evoke more from us. . . . Only when we join with others do our gifts become visible, even to ourselves. . . . . People . . . call them miracles.[13]

Jenee's son is a healer, though not in the ways most of us would anticipate—or sometimes welcome. By being who he is, he stretches our images of who we are and who we are called to be.

The Pain of Divine Healing in Communities

Communities, churches, and other groups often need divine healing; and the process of healing may be similar to the surgical healing my friend Fran describes as she makes an analogy to scrubbing her son's burns in order to bring healing. She often tells her story to remind others that God can work to bring healing through words or actions we may not welcome. She and I were among those who became clergywomen at a time when we were not always welcome in the church. I fear that our very presence felt like painful scrubbing of tender skin to some of our sisters and brothers in Christ, and we grieved the pain.

We live still in a broken world, and brokenness continues to live in our churches. I yearn for healing, and I hurt each time a sister or brother must scrub away my old skin that keeps me from being part of the healing reign that God is bringing. I hurt each time I believe I am called to dispense a gift of scrubbing away the old skin of others. If I am faithful to the Hebrew prophetic tradition, I find no joy in this painful scrubbing on the way to health. I weep as my friend Fran did as she scrubbed her beloved son. Sisters and brothers in Christ weep together in our brokenness and do not shrink from painful scrubbing. The biblical prophets often lamented as they proclaimed judgment on the people.[14] Such lament undergirds these words from the prophet Jeremiah:

> I brought you into a plentiful land
> to eat its fruits and its good things.
> But when you entered you defiled my land,
> and made my heritage an abomination.
> —Jeremiah 2:7

I recall the pain-filled courage and anger of an African American clergy-woman, who made time to speak hard words to me. In a lecture, I attempted to honor one I loved by taking her out of invisibility and naming her shaping of my life. My angry sister in Christ taught me that my privilege of "two mothers" was at her expense. Her mother had worked for "a white family like yours. She could not be there for me as she ached to be. And you dare to talk about two mothers!" It hurt me to hear her words. It was a pain-filled scrubbing away of another layer of my limited understanding of our tortured racial history. I no longer tell my story that way; my sister's words brought healing I did not know I required, had not sought, and in the moment, did not welcome. She stripped away my illusion of my "progress" and "sensitivity."

We Need One Another

> God could have made us perfect,
> but God chose not to so we would need one another.

Meredith has come home. At first, she exhibited the opposite of the self-sufficiency she had tried to invent. She came home and became like a child who needed tender mothering from Elisabeth. She was very tired. After a while, it was time to contribute to the life of the family, and Meredith began to look for a job and share the responsibilities of the household. Elisabeth relates that there have been moments that sound to me like "painful scrubbing." Healing is beginning.

The prayer of Michel Bouttier with which we end each chapter is from a collection of prayers he wrote when he was a young pastor in a small commu-

47

> Examine your experiences with sisters and brothers in Christ. Have you had experiences in which the words of another felt like painful scrubbing? Are there times you have been called to speak those hard words? By what criteria do you discern whether you are seeking to heal or only to hurt?

nity in France. (He is now retired, having had a distinguished career at a French seminary teaching New Testament.) I often use sections from this collection when I work with groups of students, clergy, or laity to remind us that our studying and working and praying lives are never in isolation. These prayers remind us that we are bound to those in our villages—our congregational village and other "villages" of which we are a part.

Closing
Sing two or three times in closing: "Come and Fill Our Hearts." Then join in these prayers:

O God, . . . take the chaos and confusion and disorder of our minds and spirits and hold them so completely in Thy grasp that the impure thing will become pure, . . . and the crass and hard thing will be gentled by Thy spirit. . . . Amen.[15]

—Howard Thurman

And, Lord, never let me sleep until I have stretched my hands over my village and invoked your blessings on it. . . . Amen.[16]

—Michel Bouttier

Notes

1. "Come and Fill Our Hearts" can be found in *The Faith We Sing* (Nashville: Abingdon Press, 2000), number 2157.

2. Samuel H. Miller, *Prayers for Daily Use* (New York: Harper & Brothers Publishers, 1957), page 90. Your group may prefer to pray this adaptation:
Center us down, O God, until in our deepest soul we kneel, quietly, waitfully, reverently. Deliver us from the world for these brief moments, so that we may meet [you] undistractedly, and confirm the bond that binds us to [you]. Then in [your] presence help us to reorder our minds and hearts, bringing before[you] one by

one our loved ones, our hopes and fears, our great joys and our ill-admitted sins, until we see with [your] eyes and love with [your] grace.

3. Richard Wright, *Black Boy* (New York: Harper & Row, 1966), page 88. Richard Wright was a novelist and short-story author. He was one of the first African American writers to protest white American treatment of black Americans. Best known are his novel *Native Son* (1940) and a memoir, *Black Boy* (1945).

4. *Catherine of Siena: The Dialogue,* translated and introduction by Suzanne Noffke, O.P.; preface by Giuliana Cavallini (New York: Paulist Press, 1980), page 38.

5. *Julian of Norwich: Showings,* translated and introduction by Edmund Colledge and James Walsh; preface by Jean Leclercq (New York: Paulist Press, 1978), page 301.

6. *Julian of Norwich,* page 302.

7. Margaret Wheatley and Myron Kellner-Rogers, *A Simpler Way* (San Francisco: Berrett-Koehler Publishing, 1996), page 44. Margaret Wheatley invites us to learn from the way all life organizes itself. She suggests that we may discover new models for our ways of being with one another by looking, for example, at "the new science" of chaos theory and quantum physics. See especially *Leadership and the New Science* and *A Simpler Way.*

8. *A Simpler Way,* page 53.

9. Susan Sonnenday Vogel, *And Then Mark Died: Letters of Grief, Love, and Faith* (Nashville: Abingdon Press, 2003), page 109.

10. Pamela Gibson Bauer, "Is God a Serial Killer?" unpublished manuscript. (Pam's title comes from her despair over people saying things like, "God must have a plan we do not understand," or "We do not know why God would take someone so young.")

11. Jenee has lived her calling as a scholar through developing a Web site called *The Text This Week: Lectionary, Scripture Study, and Worship Links and Resources* at *www.textweek.com.* You can read about Philip and his sister, Jaie, within the Web site at *www.textweek.com/jaie_and_philip.htm.* The story of "Phil's Christmas" offers a poignant window into the lives of Phil, Jenee, and their family.

12. E-mail to author from Jenee Woodard.

13. *A Simpler Way,* page 67.

14. For a discussion of the prophets lamenting as they proclaim judgment, see Walter Brueggeman, *The Prophetic Imagination* (Philadelphia: Fortress Press, 1978).

15. Howard Thurman, *The Centering Moment* (New York: Harper & Row, 1969), page 112.

16. Michel Bouttier, *Prayers for My Village* (Nashville: Upper Room Books, 1994), page 58.

CHAPTER 4
"ASK, AND IT WILL BE GIVEN"

Does prayer make a difference in healing?

Focus: This chapter explores prayer as gift from God, a means of grace, and an opportunity to experience divine healing through the experience of God's presence and through God's reordering and re-forming of our minds and hearts and restoring right relationships with others.

> **Gathering**
> Sing together two or three times "Come and Fill Our Hearts."[1] Then join together in prayer:
>
> *Center us down, O God, until in our deepest soul we kneel, quietly, waitfully, reverently. Deliver us from the world for these brief moments, so that we may meet thee undistractedly, and confirm the bond that binds us to thee. Then in thy presence help us to reorder our minds and hearts, bringing before thee one by one our loved ones, our hopes and fears, our great joys and our ill-admitted sins, until we see with thine eyes and love with thy grace.*[2]
>
> After a few moments of silence, lift concerns for healing that are on your hearts. All respond in prayer: *We bring this care before you.*
> Close with these words: *Help us to reorder our minds and hearts, until we see with your eyes and love with your grace. Amen.*

Just Ask

Ask, and it will be given you; search, and you will find; knock, and the door will be opened for you.

—Matthew 7:7

God does nothing but in answer to prayer; and even they who have been converted to God, without praying for it themselves (which is exceeding rare), were not without the prayers of others. Every new victory which a soul gains is the effect of a new prayer.[3]

—John Wesley

So certain are these words that Matthew says Jesus spoke to his disciples, and how sure John Wesley sounds as he writes of prayer. Are these words intended to bring comfort to us who are in need of healing? Are they meant to be reassuring for us who ache with the pain of our sisters and brothers? We do not know what was intended, but the effect of these admonitions may be frightening, rather than reassuring; confusing, rather than comforting. As I see on television this morning the devastation wrought by one small car bomb, and as I weep with the student who has again discovered a suspicious lump in her breast, I wonder what these words can mean. My student has a diligent prayer community that surrounds her; and yet, she keeps returning to the hospital. Congregations of every faith pray that healing will come to the brokenness of that land we call "holy," but mothers and fathers on every side still watch their children die. One dare not exclaim, "What else can possibly go wrong?!"

"Ask, and it will be given you. . . ." Is that not what we have been doing—asking and begging and pleading that God will heal and comfort and reconcile and make new? Yes, there are some who know healing. In a few places of the world, fighting ends and rebuilding begins. A young widow haltingly begins to discover that she can go on. But what can it possibly mean for the words in Matthew to continue: "For *everyone* who asks receives, and *everyone* who searches finds, and for

> Find one or two others in your group. Talk about occasions in your life when you prayed "hard" for a person or situation. Were there times when you felt that your prayer made a difference? Were there times when you doubted that your prayer made a difference? Did you ever become discouraged? Tell one another your responses.

51

> Spend time reflecting on Matthew 7:7-8. Consult a good Bible commentary like *The New Interpreter's Bible.* What insights emerge in your study and reflection?

everyone who knocks, the door will be opened" (7:8, italics added)? And what can John Wesley mean with his strange words? the great God of the universe cannot, or will not, act apart from our prayers? It is not only confusing. It feels like a massive burden on my shoulders. If so much is wrong, does that mean I, and my sisters and brothers, have not been asking and searching? Are we responsible—and guilty?

Prayer—A Means of Grace

It helps to remember that John Wesley considered prayer to be one of the "means of grace." It is a gift. Through the centuries and millennia of religion-making, men and women have searched for the formula, the magic, or the secret that would connect them with their gods. *Our* God has offered to us the gift of prayer and promised it is a means of grace and an assurance of God's presence to us and with us.

> How many still look to "the pastor" to offer every prayer? Do some still see only the priest's prayer as efficacious? What might happen if we would reclaim the awareness of prayer as a gift given for all of God's people?

Wesleyan scholar Randy Maddox has observed that—although John Wesley was very clear that prayer and other means of grace were gifts of God—it did not take very long for followers to turn the gifts into "duties." They became things we *had* to do, and certain ones—the professional religious people—had particular responsibility for doing them.[4]

The Prayers of Samuel Miller

Consider the prayer of Samuel Miller that has been offered for the opening of each chapter. Think about the content of that prayer:

Center us down, O God, until in our deepest soul we kneel, quietly, waitfully, reverently. Deliver us from the world for these brief moments, so that we may meet thee undistractedly, and confirm the bond that binds us to thee. Then in thy presence help us to reorder our minds and hearts, bring-

ing before thee one by one our loved ones, our hopes and fears, our great joys and our ill-admitted sins, until we see with thine eyes and love with thy grace.[5]

The prayer asks that God center us *until* we reach that place of waiting and anticipation. It prays that we may pull away from all other things (not for long, but for these moments), *so that* we might meet God anew and confirm our bond with God. It prays for the reordering of our

> Read Samuel Miller's prayer two or three times. Think about the requests in the prayer. List them. How do you think this prayer might offer divine healing?

minds and hearts . . . *until*, finally, we see with God's eyes and love with God's grace.

Samuel Miller's prayers have helped me to know prayer as a gift, and his own prayers have been treasures for me. A surface reading of Miller's résumé might make one think he is an unlikely resource for exploring the depths of prayer and healing. Born in 1900, Miller prepared to become a Baptist preacher and served several small congregations without great success, by the world's standards. Although he never earned a Ph.D. degree, he was named dean of Harvard Divinity School, wrote several books, and lectured widely.

What is it that makes Samuel Miller's prayers treasures for many? What can they teach about prayer and healing? Pause for a time to pray these selected lines from his prayers:

O God, within us there are prayers that know no words; . . . sorrows that stand forever in silence before thy face, humbled by a mystery in which light and darkness are mingled deeper than our sight; . . . remembrances that lay their hallowing hands on all hours with a benediction sweeter than peace. Hear us, O God, though we do not speak.[6]

Thou who standest beyond both the darkness and the light, who art hidden by the names we give thee, and who movest in mystery to touch us to life, . . . undeceive us, and bring us where we will find that thou art our Savior and our Lord.[7]

[O]ur words are often poor and wingless, stumbling from our hearts like strangers, yet always we wait for the time when even our anguish and silence will be touched by healing glory, and we will be one with thee in peace and joy.[8]

> Reflect silently on these prayers. What parts speak to your heart? What do they say about what prayer is? What do these prayers suggest to you about divine healing?

Holy thou art, O gracious Father, ministering to our little lives through unending mysteries and luring us patiently by a thousand paths into an abundant life; . . .[9]

From this short selection, you can see the remarkable capacity Miller had for choosing words and creating images that bring forth that which may be unformed within us. When he does not find an adequate word, he invents one. He has a way of helping me say what I did not know I felt—or what I failed to see I was being called to be.

It was long after I had begun praying Samuel Miller's prayers that I discovered the tragic parts of his life and history—that as a young child, he experienced the death of his brother, and that he lost two sons in World War II. It was then I understood why his prayers touched my own life so tenderly and drew me toward healing and new life. *He knew.* He knew pain and suffering. He knew the isolation. He knew that it grew worse before it could begin to be better. His prayer "In time of death" ends:

Though the pain deepens, keep us in thy way and guide us past every danger, through Jesus Christ our Lord.[10]

> What do you think "prayer can be in times of pain and hardship"? Write a prayer that reflects your thoughts.

Samuel Miller can be a resource for prayer and healing because he knows. He knows suffering, and he takes us through his prayers into an understanding of what prayer can be in times of pain and hardship.

I see in these prayers an awareness that all of us know suffering. Miller's own was always upon him—not only his grief over the loss of those dear to him, but also his heavy sorrow over the state of the world. There was his sense of unfitness for some of the work he was called to do and his dis-ease with the life of the church in his day. In the church of the 1950s, his vision and the reality of the church were often far distant from each other. Yet, he loved the people; he grieved with them and for them.[11]

The Small Word *Until*

For me, Miller's prayers witness to the assurance that God has offered prayer to us as a gift—a promise that through prayer we do enter into God's presence and renew that bond that will lead us to re-order, re-shape, re-form all of who we are. Prayer is at the heart of Christian formation, and Miller prays always with conviction that re-formation will happen. Repeatedly in his prayers is that precious small word *until*. In our opening prayer, he prays with the assurance that God will help us reorder our whole selves "*until* we see with thine eyes and love with thy grace" (italics added).

Bind together one by one the vagrant impulses of our goodness and every holy desire, *until* we do thy will in all things, through Jesus Christ our Lord [italics added]. [12]

. . . steady us, *until* we lift up our eyes unto thee, and know our hope is in thee, both now and forever [italics added].[13]

I hear confidence. I am called to wait on our God with assurance— *until*—I live in God's presence. That is what prayer is. "Wherever [I] walk, in sunshine or in shadow," I walk as one who lives in God's presence.[14]

The Corporate Nature of Healing Prayer

Yet, that does not say it as he would, for "my" prayer is "our" prayer. It is always "we" who are praying, whether we are gathered as a body in worship or meditating in front of the fireplace, walking a forest path or weeping in the lonely hospital chapel. I am "we." I am bound with sisters and brothers in Christ. Together we live in God's presence.

I have found Eugene Peterson's work on the Psalms a helpful resource in understanding the corporate nature of prayer. Peterson suggests that the Psalms are "God's gift to train us in prayer that is comprehensive . . . and honest. . . ."[15] "By ourselves, we are not ourselves. . . . Individuals don't 'make up' the community, they are produced by it. . . . We are part of something before we are anything, and never more so than when we pray."[16]

> How do you understand the corporate nature of prayer? What is it like for you to pray in groups? to pray alone? How do you think praying alone can be a form of corporate prayer?

Peterson's entire book is a useful resource for the study of the Psalms as tools for prayer, "not tools for doing or getting, but for being and becoming,"[17] "the center where Christ worked in his praying."[18]

Entering the Shadows

We pray in the presence of the One who, in Christ, has known every suffering we could ever know—pain and hunger, loneliness and betrayal, rejection and radical misunderstanding, grief and the awareness of imminent death. Miller's prayers invite all of us to recognize and enter into the shadow sides of our lives, the hard places.

[I]f we are spiritually discouraged or in despair let us not come before thee in the semblance of faith put on, as if our pain or perplexity were not real.[19]

[I]f we deny our own darkness and cover it with bright words, be patient, O Lord, and wait until we are stronger.[20]

Miller invites me to see that God's presence is a safe place—a place I can dare to recognize and name the suffering within my heart, the pain carried by the community around me, the brokenness of the whole world. That presence is the place where I can grow strong enough to be able to recognize the suffering; for I dare not even name it if I do not have some assurance that another surrounds me and will not leave me alone with my suffering.

> Read the contemporary *Psalms of Lament* that Ann Weems wrote in the years following the murder of her son. Like the biblical psalms, these prayer poems take the reader into the depth of grief-filled agony, and the closing words of each prayer look forward with assurance and hope.[21]

Another thoughtful student of prayer, Kathleen Norris, guides me to related learning from the Psalms as she explains what a Benedictine sister taught her:

[The Psalms] defeat our tendency to try to be holy without being human first. . . .

The psalms make us uncomfortable because they don't allow us to deny either the depth of our pain or the possibility of its transformation into praise.[22]

The insight of this wise sister, carved out of her living with the Psalms, reflects the understanding I see in Miller's prayers. He will not let me deny my suffering or the suffering of those around me. He makes me recognize the pain of injustice that I did not yet know to be pain. But he does not let me stay there.

> How do you describe the "shadows" in your life? How can prayer help you face such shadows? What potential do you see for divine healing in your willingness to pray about such shadows or to confront them in God's presence?

> Particular help for entering into the shadow sides and hard places of our lives comes from the prayers of African American Christians, whose corporate journey has been one of persistence in the face of suffering. Look, for example, at *Guide My Feet* by Marian Wright Edelman, a collection that addresses especially concerns about children; the writings of Howard Thurman, such as *The Centering Moment* or *Meditations of the Heart; Conversations with God: Two Centuries of Prayers by African Americans,* edited by James Melvin Washington; *An African Prayer Book,* edited by Bishop Desmond Tutu, which includes prayers from the continent of Africa and those of African Americans.[23]

Something Happens That Makes a Difference

When I am in God's presence, praying Samuel Miller's prayers, I expect something to happen that will make a difference.

Because I am always "we," prayer binds me together with sisters and brothers in a covenant of intertwined prayer. We are praying for one another, and we are the ones for whom others are praying. Even when we do not know how to do that praying, we are promised that the Spirit intercedes for us (Romans 8:26).

It is my own experience, during my worst hours and days and months of suffering, that I had a palpable sense of being carried by the prayers of the community of faith. I have heard others who are grieving or in trauma or grave illness use the same words. Through prayer, God not only renews the

> How would you describe the "something happens that makes a difference" in your prayer life? How is it connected to divine healing?

bonds that bind us to God's own self, but we can come to know ourselves as part of the whole body. Something happens that makes a difference.

Reordering Our Minds and Hearts

In Samuel Miller's prayer at the beginning of the chapter, an integral part of "reordering our minds and hearts . . . until we see with [God's] eyes and love with [God's] grace," is bringing into God's presence all that is on our hearts and minds—"our loved ones, our hopes and fears, our great joys and ill-admitted sins."

> Ask, and it will be given you; search, and you will find; knock, and the door will be opened for you.
>
> —Matthew 7:7

> God does nothing but in answer to prayer; and even they who have been converted to God, without praying for it themselves (which is exceeding rare), were not without the prayers of others. Every new victory which a soul gains is the effect of a new prayer.[24]
>
> —John Wesley

What is the connection between that for which we ask and that which is given? I cannot forget that the one who is making the promise is also described as the one whose power works within us "to accomplish abundantly far more than all we can ask or imagine" (Ephesians 3:20).

It has become commonplace to say that prayer is not intended to change God but to change us. Yet, I wonder if it might be said that prayer re-forms our *relationship* with God, and thus changes who we are with God and who we are in relation to others. Dare I imagine that in the changing of the relationship, prayer changes also who God is with us and with those for whom we pray? As I pray, morning after morning after morning, this prayer that has been our opening each chapter, I pray with a growing assurance that God is re-ordering our minds and hearts—not just my own, but, potentially, all of ours.

How does that re-ordering happen? Could it be that it happens as we all ask and search and knock—bringing before God "one by one, our loved ones, our hopes and fears, our great joys and ill-

---

Review the discussions of relationships in Chapter 3. See especially the quotations from Margaret Wheatley that say that all is relationship. What are the implications here for our relationship with God and others in prayer?

admitted sins"? It sounds as if Samuel Miller is inviting us to pray with him in the assurance that it is *through this asking and seeking* that we are made to see with God's eyes and love with God's grace, and learning to see with God's eyes and love with God's grace is a part of the process of divine healing.

As Miller prays for those "in dire extremity," he calls upon God as the "Refuge of our bewildered hearts" and with the assurance that "within the shadow of our fears thy love doth stand waiting upon the very threshold of our need." And then he goes on with these words:

> Help us to pray for those whom we love, that we may commend them to thy care, not alone by the anxiety of our affection but by our faith that thou also dost take *delight* in them whom we remember and will shepherd their days and nights with a *wisdom* and a *love* greater than our own [italics added].[25]

Could it be that our prayers for healing—for ourselves and others— move us toward seeing and loving ourselves and the others for whom we pray with the *delight and wisdom and love* that God has for us, for all of us? Could it be that as our minds and hearts are re-formed in prayer, in part through our asking and seeking, we come each day into a new relationship with God and God with us? Could it be that then there emerge from our prayers new ways of our being with ourselves and others that *is* healing?

Paul may have had this connection in mind in Philippians 4:6-7. One translation (NEB) says:

> The Lord is near; have no anxiety, but in everything make your requests known to God in prayer and petition with thanksgiving. *Then* the peace of God, which is beyond our utmost understanding, will keep guard over your hearts and your thoughts, in Christ Jesus [italics added].

Make your petitions known to God, and *then* God will keep guard over your hearts and thoughts.

Prayer as Healing Experience

I know that I am alive today—in body and spirit—because in my hardest times I was carried by the prayers of people of faith, people and communities whose lives intertwined with mine in ways I will never be able

59

> Try praying an "enacted prayer" in your group. Lift a concern for intercessory prayer. Imagine, for example, you are praying for a young mother who is being treated for cancer. Assign one person to be the young mother, another to be her child, another to be her doctor, another perhaps to be a caring church member, and two or three others to represent God. Enact your prayer. What is your prayer for the doctor in relation to the mother? What about the child? What will you ask God to do in relation to each? Those who work with enacted prayer start by stating clearly, "This is a real prayer." The difference is that it is done with your bodies instead of words.

to understand. I know they prayed because they told me—told me in tender words, in poignant notes, in telephone calls long after others had forgotten. During those days I did not feel a need to explore how it was that healing came through that praying. I experienced it. And that led me to respond with a commitment to pray for those I knew to be in need of healing, and to tell them.[26]

God has never required that we "understand" the gifts and practices that have been offered to us as means of grace. We are not called to say how they "work." Some theologians spend their lives attempting that, and there are times in each of our lives when we are likely to feel driven to figure it out. But our receiving the means of grace is not contingent on our explaining them.

Recently, some have found it important to "test" the power of prayer. See, for example, an article in *Parade Magazine,* March 23, 2003, by Dianne Hales entitled, "Why Prayer Could Be Good Medicine."[27] Larry Dossey, M.D., is well known for his writing about the healing potential of prayer. His books include *Prayer Is Good Medicine: How to Reap the Healing Benefits of Prayer* and *Healing Words: The Power of Prayer and the Practice of Medicine.*[28] Some may want to explore these studies. A conversation about the results and the reasons some find this approach important could be a clarifying exercise.

> Read one of Larry Dossey's books or the article by Dianne Hales in *Parade.* What is your response to using the tools of science to explore connections between prayer and healing?

Healing Prayer as Listening

Ask, and it will be given you; search, and you will find; knock, and the door will be opened for you. —Matthew 7:7

For most of us, the "asking" and "searching" and "knocking" may be the most familiar forms of our prayer. But if the receiving and the opening of the door are to be a part of our experience of prayer and healing, beyond all we can ask or imagine, then the practices of silence and listening will be required.

> Spend some moments in the silence. How is it for you when you are alone? when you are in a group? How do you think such moments of silence can offer divine healing?

Uncrowd our hearts, O God, until silence speaks in thy still small voice; turn us from the hearing of words, and the making of words, and the confusion of much speaking, that we may possess ourselves for these brief moments undistracted, waiting, with all our hopes listening for thy footfall. Amen.[29]

Silence is an uncommon experience for many of us and may feel "unnatural." For some personality types, silence comes more easily than for others. For some, "listening" may happen more easily through *lectio divina* (or holy reading), using Scripture or other readings from various parts of our traditions.

Some listen best in the context of the natural world and others, through forms of the arts. One practice that may be helpful for listening is guided imagery. Flora Slosson Wuellner has written *Feed*

> **Lectio Divina**
>
> *Lectio divina* can be done in different ways. You can find descriptions in many spiritual formation resources. One approach that comes from the Benedictine tradition invites you, first, to read the passage slowly and listen deeply. Second, meditate on the passage. Think about words; fill your mind with the Word. Third, let the Scripture draw you into prayer; and, fourth, simply be present. Rest in the love of God you have experienced in the Scriptures. A woman who was leading my covenant group in this process captured the sense of each stage this way: Read yourself full. Think yourself clear. Pray yourself empty. Let yourself go.[30]

61

My Shepherds as a plea to church leaders to attend to their own spiritual health. It can be instructive for all God's people, not only the designated leaders. This text includes, at the end of each chapter, guided imagery exercises that are appropriate for groups or for persons to use alone.[31]

Practicing Prayer

Learning the craft of prayer means practicing, and often that is best done at first by living in the prayers of others. Explore the resources for prayer in collections such as the *A Guide to Prayer for All Who Seek God,* prepared by United Methodist bishop Rueben Job and Norman Shawchuck; *The Complete Book of Christian Prayer;* or *The Westminster Collection of Christian Prayers.*[34]

Among the wise words of Samuel Miller is his admonition, "Quit dressing your soul in somebody else's piety."[32] Each of us will discover and create our own ways of asking and listening. At the same time, we are not without resources and practices that have shaped people of faith through the centuries; and Miller reminds me that I have to practice doing what I do not yet know how to do. That is the way I have learned *every* craft and practice—cooking, dancing, and now praying and listening.[33]

Healing Happens

One of the most common words in Samuel Miller's prayers, and in much of his other writing, is *mystery*. He does not write as if any of us can understand or figure out prayer. He was willing to live in the mystery—and invite companions in prayer to join him there. As I join him there, I live increasingly in the assurance that healing happens as together we ask and search and knock. Healing happens as we listen and know the re-ordering of our minds and hearts. Healing happens as we are bound into intertwining covenants of prayer with our sisters and brothers and with God.

Notes

1. "Come and Fill Our Hearts" can be found in *The Faith We Sing* (Nashville: Abingdon Press, 2000), number 2157.

2. Samuel H. Miller, *Prayers for Daily Use* (New York: Harper & Brothers Publishers, 1957), page 90. Your group may prefer to pray this adaptation:
Center us down, O God, until in our deepest soul we kneel, quietly, waitfully, rev-

Closing
Sing two or three times in closing: "Come and Fill Our Hearts." Then join in these prayers:

O God, . . . take the chaos and confusion and disorder of our minds and spirits and hold them so completely in Thy grasp that the impure thing will become pure, . . . and the crass and hard thing will be gentled by Thy spirit. . . . Amen.[35]
—Howard Thurman

*And, Lord, never let me sleep until
I have stretched my hands over my village
and invoked your blessings on it. . . . Amen.*[36]
—Michel Bouttier

erently. Deliver us from the world for these brief moments, so that we may meet [you] undistractedly, and confirm the bond that binds us to [you]. Then in [your] presence help us to reorder our minds and hearts, bringing before[you] one by one our loved ones, our hopes and fears, our great joys and our ill-admitted sins, until we see with [your] eyes and love with [your] grace.

3. John Wesley, *A Plain Account of Christian Perfection*, ¶25, Q. 38, §5, *Works* (Jackson) 11:437.

4. Maddox presented these insights during the conference "Forming Christian Leaders" April 30 – May 2, 1999, at the Claremont School of Theology, in Claremont CA. Other resources by Maddox that might add to our Wesleyan foundations are: Randy L. Maddox, *Rethinking Wesley's Theology for Contemporary Methodism* (Nashville: Abingdon Press, 2003); Randy L. Maddox, *Responsible Grace: John Wesley's Practical Theology* (Nashville: Abingdon Press, 1994); Randy L. Maddox, *Aldersgate Reconsidered* (Nashville: Abingdon Press, 1990); Randy L. Maddox and Diane Leclerc, *Singleness of Heart: Gender, Sin, and Holiness in Historical Perspective (Pietist and Wesleyan Studies, 13)* Rowan & Littlefield, 2001).

5. *Prayers for Daily Use*, page 90.
6. *Prayers for Daily Use*, page 10.
7. *Prayers for Daily Use*, page 27.
8. *Prayers for Daily Use*, page 31.
9. *Prayers for Daily Use*, page 35.
10. *Prayers for Daily Use*, page 128.
11. Ernst E. Klein, *Samuel H. Miller: Honest Man of God*, unpublished manuscript.
12. *Prayers for Daily Use*, page 33.
13. *Prayers for Daily Use*, page 31.
14. *Prayers for Daily Use*, page 126.
15. Eugene H. Peterson, *Answering God: The Psalms as Tools for Prayer* (San Francisco: Harper & Row, 1989), page 3.

16. *Answering God,* pages 18, 84.

17. *Answering God,* page 2.

18. *Answering God,* page 4.

19. *Prayers for Daily Use,* page 66.

20. *Prayers for Daily Use,* page 34.

21. Ann Weems, *Psalms of Lament* (Louisville, KY: Westminster John Knox Press, 1995).

22. Kathleen Norris, *The Cloister Walk* (New York: Riverhead Books, 1996), page 96.

23. Marian Wright Edelman, *Guide My Feet: Prayers and Meditations on Loving and Working for Children* (Boston: Beacon Press, 1995); Howard Thurman, *The Centering Moment* (New York: Harper & Row, 1969); Howard Thurman, *Meditations of the Heart* (Boston: Beacon Press, 1999); James Melvin Washington, ed. *Conversations with God: Two Centuries of Prayers by African Americans* (New York: HarperCollins, 1994); Bishop Desmond Tutu, selected and with an introduction by, *An African Prayer Book* (New York: Doubleday, 1995).

24. *A Plain Account of Christian Perfection,* ¶25, Q. 38, §5, *Works* (Jackson) 11:437.

25. *Prayers for Daily Use,* page 126.

26. Susan Sonnenday Vogel, *And Then Mark Died: Letters of Grief, Love, and Faith* (Nashville: Abingdon Press, 2003), pages 89–98. In two of the letters in *And Then Mark Died,* I describe in detail the power of those prayers and the practices in my own life that were shaped by that experience.

27. Dianne Hales, "Why Prayer Could Be Good Medicine" *Parade Magazine,* 23 March 2003, pages 4–5.

28. Larry Dossey, M.D., *Prayer Is Good Medicine: How to Reap the Healing Benefits of Prayer* (San Francisco: HarperSanFrancisco, 1996); *Healing Words: The Power of Prayer and the Practice of Medicine* (New York: HarperCollins, 1993).

29. *Prayers for Daily Use,* page 35.

30. From material prepared and taught by Mary Jo Polak, OSB.

31. Flora Slosson Wuellner, *Feed My Shepherds: Spiritual Healing and Renewal for Those in Christian Leadership* (Nashville: Upper Room Books, 1998).

32. Samuel H. Miller, *The Life of the Soul* (New York: Harper & Row, 1951), page 21.

33. *The Life of the Soul,* pages 16–17.

34. Norman Shawchuck and Rueben Job, *A Guide to Prayer for All Who Seek God* (Nashville: Upper Room Books, 2003); Dorothy M. Stewart, compiler, *The Westminster Collection of Christian Prayers* (Louisville, KY: Westminster John Knox Press, 2002); *The Complete Book of Christian Prayer* (New York: Continuum, 1995).

35. Howard Thurman, *The Centering Moment* (New York: Harper & Row, 1969), page 112.

36. Michel Bouttier, *Prayers for My Village* (Nashville: Upper Room Books, 1994), page 58.

CHAPTER 5
"LOSE THEIR LIFE FOR MY SAKE"?

Will we seek healing if we believe
we should suffer?

Focus: This chapter explores how some ways of viewing self-denial and suffering can interfere with divine healing. God's desire is for healing and wholeness. God in Christ stands with us and strengthens us in times of suffering.

Gathering
Sing together two or three times "Come and Fill Our Hearts."[1] Then join together in prayer:

Center us down, O God, until in our deepest soul we kneel, quietly, waitfully, reverently. Deliver us from the world for these brief moments, so that we may meet thee undistractedly, and confirm the bond that binds us to thee. Then in thy presence help us to reorder our minds and hearts, bringing before thee one by one our loved ones, our hopes and fears, our great joys and our ill-admitted sins, until we see with thine eyes and love with thy grace. [2]

After a few moments of silence, lift concerns for healing that are on your hearts. All respond in prayer: *We bring this care before you.*
Close with these words: *Help us to reorder our minds and hearts, until we see with your eyes and love with your grace. Amen.*

Self-denial and Divine Healing

If any want to become my followers, let them deny themselves and take up their cross and follow . . . [T]hose who lose their life for my sake . . . will save it.

—Mark 8:34-35

Is my life only valuable if I give it away? Am I called always to put others' concerns before my own? What will that mean for healing? Will I seek healing if I believe I am supposed to suffer?

It was the spring of 2002. I was sixty years old. I had read and studied theology for over forty years and taught in related fields for thirty. My thinking and believing life had taken several turns during those years and was now settled, I thought. People often asked if the loss of my son had shaken my beliefs, and I could honestly say that Mark's death had deepened my life of faith.

Then one Saturday I read a book that dislodged my theological moorings. The context intensified my response: The day before, I had visited my friend in a psychiatric ward and heard her anguish over past abuse and the demons that haunt her still. She had tried before to take her own life; this time she nearly accomplished it. Then I listened to a life-long friend describe her suffering in the face of her husband's betrayal. If she really loved him, he told her, she would understand.

As I completed the book, I found that not only was I intellectually adrift; I was emotionally and spiritually splintered. The book I had read described the ways in which our theologies about the work of Christ have been used to make Christian women, and some men as well, believe they should find their fulfillment in suffering. If we are going to be faithful, we should not leave situations that bring suffering. I should rejoice in my sufferings, for they make me Christ-like and bring me closer to Jesus.

The book was *Proverbs of Ashes* by Rita Nakashima Brock and Rebecca Parker.[3] It is haunting, filled with the pain and suffering of women whose faith often kept them locked in situations of abuse or encouraged them to make choices that did not lead to healing.

If any want to become my followers, let them deny themselves and take up their cross and follow . . . those who lose their life for my sake . . . will save it.

—Mark 8:34-35

66

The book and my friends' pain led me into crisis. I am told that crisis can mean opportunity, but that was difficult to foresee in those days and weeks of agonizing bewilderment. What was I going to do? How could I teach? How could I serve Communion? How was I going to provide guidance for students who looked to me? I discovered myself in a terrifying wilderness, and I could not speak about my confusion without tears.

> Read Mark 8:34-35. How do you respond to this call to self-denial? How does it challenge you?
> Now, read Mark 8:27-33. What is the context or circumstance in the Scripture that prompts the teaching? What was happening in the biblical account? How do the events in the story shape the teaching?

A Letter to Julian of Norwich

During my morning quiet time, I was re-reading one of Samuel Miller's books and came upon words that sounded as if he were speaking directly to my heart:

> Make a totally new start. Get rid of everything upon which you have been leaning and start all over again. . . . [R]efresh yourself and dig a new well somewhere.[4]

I took steps toward finding a new well when our family had the opportunity for a study leave in England. While there, my husband and I went one afternoon to the location of the cell where Julian of Norwich lived for twenty years and where she wrote of her visions.

Julian of Norwich was an anchoress who lived in solitude in Norwich in the late fourteenth century. She received sixteen revelations of God's love, which she called "showings." She recorded these revelations in a short version and, later, after further prayer and reflection, in a longer version.[5]

My husband and I sat quietly in Julian's cell. Stuart lit a candle. In the stillness, I listened and prayed and imagined what Julian might have experienced there. I wanted to speak with her. In those moments, and in the days that followed, I imagined what I would write to her:

My dear sister in Christ,

For years I knew you only as our foremother in the faith who offered us the lovely image of "our Kind Mother Jesus." In the early years of "the women's movement" of our time, it was a surprising blessing to discover your words. Then, in my hardest hours, I read the assurance you had recorded as Jesus' promise to you, "All will be well, and all will be well, and all manner of thing will be well." I knew comfort. You have known what it is to be in pain and confusion. You will understand.

My heart is breaking for my sisters in Christ who live with suffering and abuse. I want them to know healing. I want them to *want* healing. My heart is full of anger because of the ways the church you and I love has exacerbated their suffering rather than requiring justice and offering messages that engender healing. Let me tell you what I have heard and read.

Pastor Rebecca tells of Anola and her abusive husband. He was jailed for beating her. Then she let him come home. It might mean pain and violence; but, she thought, "A good woman would be willing to accept personal pain, and think only of the good of the family. You know, 'Your life is only valuable if it's given away' and 'This is your cross to bear.' She "believed God expected her to risk being battered, like Jesus."[6] Several days later, in a rage, Anola's husband killed her.

Rebecca's friend laments that she knows the husband is responsible. "But I can't escape the feeling that he wouldn't have had the chance if the church hadn't taught Anola that your life is only valuable if you give it away."[7]

Rebecca tells also about Lucia, another abused wife. She told Rebecca that her pastor said she should stay in her marriage and "rejoice in my sufferings because they bring me closer to Jesus. He said, 'Jesus suffered because he loved us.' He said, 'If you love Jesus, accept the beatings and bear them gladly, as Jesus bore the cross.'" She asked Rebecca if her pastor was right.[8]

As Rebecca listened to Lucia's story, she remembered the sermon she had preached the past Sunday—"on the willingness of love to suffer." Rebecca had said, "love bears all things. Never breaks relationship. Keeps ties of connection to others even when they hurt you. Places the needs of the other before concern for the self."[9]

Rebecca also knew suffering and still longed for healing. She was abused as a child at the hands of a neighbor. She had learned that when she was suffering, she must not turn to her family or the church. "The good person cares for others, but if she herself is hurt, frightened, confused, or in need, these weaknesses are to be nursed in private, covered over, or solved without bothering anyone else."[10]

As Rebecca recounted the anguish of a decision she had to make, I recognized myself. Rebecca's anguish came from a set of circumstances and decisions different from mine, but I recognized the pattern. It was the familiar pattern of sacrificing what I wanted, and "then peace and security are restored, relationship is preserved, ..." Rebecca recognized that "Christianity had taught me that sacrifice is the way of life. . . . To make sacrifice or to be sacrificed is virtuous and redemptive."[11]

> What is your response to the teachings that influenced both Lucia and Rebecca? Do you know of similar stories? If you are comfortable, share them with the group.

My dear sister Julian, you knew illness and suffering in your life. You wrote that you were prepared to die.[12] As I read your words, I do not believe that you saw your illness and pain to be God's will for you. Your visions did not exalt or glorify your suffering.

I fear you would be disheartened and dismayed to enter into some of our services of worship. The prayers we pray, the hymns we sing, sometimes carry a message we may not intend. Surely we do not intend it in the way some hear it.

> "Make me a captive, Lord,
>   Force me . . . ; imprison me . . .
>   enslave [my heart] with thy matchless love. . . ."

> "Bear patiently the cross of grief and pain."

> "There's a cross for everyone, and there's a cross for me."[13]

I wonder what it has done to us, singing and listening to those words for a lifetime. I fear the message is in my bones. It has not always led me to seek healing and abundant life. It has led some away from hearing God's call and away from wholeness and health. How can I want healing if I hear that suffering brings me closer to Jesus? It matters not what was "intended." The result can be tragedy.

A creative woman with a passion for ministry found her way to seminary in mid-life. "I knew I was called, but I had a family. When I talked about going to school, they made me feel as if I was being selfish. I needed to put them first and sacrifice my own calling."

Dear sister, can that be what God wants? Is that what Scriptures about losing your life are all about? That we should hide our dreams or close our hearts to what we are called to be or to do? Love the suffering—in order to be like Jesus? Imitate the sacrifice of Jesus?

I read about Rebecca's experiences. I listened to dear friends talk about their suffering—suffering they believe is a necessary part of their lives if they are good Christians. Do they even know they are in need of healing? With Rebecca, I recall the anguish of my own decisions that denied healing and new life, that kept me in suffering because the message was in my bones. That is what has led me to despair.

I begin to take heart when I read what my friend Emilie Townes has written: "The inevitability and desirability of suffering needs to be challenged. . . . Suffering, and any discussion that accepts suffering as good, is susceptible to being shaped into a tool of oppression. . . . Suffering is outrageous."[14]

Yes. Yes. I am further heartened when I read the work of Jane McAvoy and how she understands your visions:

Suffering . . . is properly the action of God and God alone. . . . Julian is forced to realize that her earlier desire to suffer with Christ was based on a false understanding of the nature of God. Julian's mature contemplation of the passion of Christ is meant to evoke the reality of God's love for us, not the model of our love for God.[15]

For more information
Jane McAvoy's books speak through her reading of several Christian women mystics. In *The Satisfied Life,* she addresses the theologies of Julian, Catherine of Siena, and Hildegard of Bingen, among others. A companion piece, *Communion with the Friends of God,* offers Communion meditations and prayers based on her study of the women in the first book.[16]

As I reflect upon your accounts of your visions, with Jane's guidance, I see you wanting to lift us up and not allow us to live in suffering. You tell us that to feel worthless in the eyes of God is sin, and this sin keeps us from seeing and feeling the loving gaze of God upon us.[17] You have discerned that there is an unbreakable connection between our sense of unworthiness and our willingness to live in suffering. I treasure the way you talk about the unconditional love that gathers us up when we have fallen down and gotten hurt and muddy. We may be afraid and ashamed.

But then our courteous Mother does not wish us to flee away, for nothing would be less pleasing to him; but he then wants us to behave like a child. For when [a child] is distressed and frightened, it runs quickly to its mother; and if it can do no more, it calls to the mother for help with all its might. . . . The sweet gracious hands of our Mother are ready and diligent about us, . . . for he wants us to love him sweetly and trust in him meekly and greatly. And he revealed this in these gracious words: I protect you very safely.[18]

A couple of days after we visited the place where you lived and prayed, we attended evening prayer at a nearby church. We prayed ancient words of confession,

We are not worthy to be called your children.
And there is no health in us.

You will smile when you hear that Stuart leaned over and whispered, "I don't think Julian and I believe that." We had come to see that you had something else to teach us about the ways God wants to care for us—and how Jesus wants to hold us and bring us healing, not suffering. We are not worthless. We *are* called to confession, but sometimes that means confessing that we do not think of ourselves as highly as we ought to think. Our confession of sin may need to include:

We confess our doubt that Jesus' healing love and abundant life are intended for us. Forgive us, and help us trust your promises.

How then, my dear sister Julian, can we understand what Jesus was saying in those hard passages about suffering to be like him? Your visions do not convey a Jesus who wants us to suffer. What can these Scriptures mean?

In one translation I have read, Jesus says, "You must come with me" (not "follow me").

Whoever cares for [one's] own safety is lost; but if [one] will let [oneself] be lost for my sake and for the Gospel, that [one] is safe. What does [one] gain by winning the whole world at the cost of [one's] true self? —Mark 8:35-36, NEB

Compare this translation to the better-known NRSV version:

For those who want to save their life will lose it, and those who lose their life for my sake, and for the sake of the gospel, will save it. For what will it profit them to gain the whole world and forfeit their life?

I wonder if the Scripture is telling us not that it was God's *will* for Jesus to suffer, but that suffering was the *result* of Jesus' faithfulness. Jesus either had to give up his true self—his true calling—and go off in fear, or he was going to keep preaching the truth—and he knew suffering was very likely to follow. He was not going to *seek* suffering. He did not want it. But he was going to be faithful to his calling.

> Read Mark 8:34-35 in several different translations of the Bible. How do additional translations inform your thinking about these difficult words? What connections do you see between this Scripture and the need for divine healing?

Maybe that means that Jesus is calling us now to live our full and true lives, not to run away in fear from that calling, but to live the dreams and visions he has put into our hearts. Suffering may come with them, for the world is not a safe place. But Christ wants for us safety and abundant life, not suffering. He is telling us that it is not suffering that makes us like him.

> Read again Mark 8:34-35, and revisit the reflection you did in the previous Bible exercises. Then consider these Scriptures in light of the Bridges material in Chapter 2. Do you see any correlations? Explore whether there is any connection between "letting go" in a transition and "losing one's life" as it is described in the Scriptures.

Jesus is calling us to come with him, to walk with him. With you, my dear sister, I hear him saying, "I will protect you very safely. I do not want suffering for you. It may find you, but I will be with you, and together we will struggle against it."

Thank you, my dear sister in Christ. Thank you for your teaching. You give me hope.

—Susan

Do We Deserve Our Suffering?

I fear another message about suffering and healing is buried deep within us and adds to our anguish. Parts of our Scripture and tradition tell us that if we are suffering, we must have done something to deserve it; we are being punished. Suffering and loss seldom are without the sting of guilt. It is hard to want and seek healing when we believe we deserve our suffering.

It is difficult to exorcise this message because it includes truth. When I was little, my mother issued the traditional mother admonition: "Do not touch the hot iron; you will get burned." Who among us did not try it once? I did what I had been told not to do, and I suffered. I ran out in the street, and I was punished. As I grew older, the admonitions and their predicted results were ominous. Do not smoke, or you will die of lung cancer or a heart attack. I saw that happen to Uncle Bill and Aunt Sue. Do not drink and drive; you will kill yourself or somebody else. Then it became more complicated.

A man I know who drinks and drives seems unaffected by the admonitions and lives without apparent consequences. A faithful and generous family loses their only child to a rare kind of tumor. This suffering family did not do anything wrong that led to their son's death. The man who does wrong has not suffered as a result. Yet, deep within us is that message that, if something terrible has happened, we must have done something wrong. Guilt compounds our suffering.

> Consider this child's response to the question "How do I know for sure that I am doing what God wants me to do?" Jeremy, age nine, answers, "If nothing bad happens to you then you know it's OK to do."[19] Do you think that would be a common answer from a child? What does that imply about popular theology?

Sometimes I *have* been wrong. It has been important for me to recognize that I could have been a better mother. That awareness goes into the large basket of regrets that every grieving person carries. It does not help when others say I did the best I could at the time. I want and seek forgiveness, and I have come to know assurance—grace upon grace. Did that wrong have a connection with my son's death? My reason says, "No," but I will never know. A character in an Ursula Hegi novel feared her effect on her children.

73

What terrified her most about being a parent was that you never knew which of your actions would affect your children for life.[20]

Do not all of my actions affect each one with whom I am in relationship? But how would I ever know the consequences of each? Is it better that I do not know? The knowledge of what brought good or healing would be a blessing, but the discovery of what brought hurt or tragedy could be unbearable.

Still there is the dilemma. It lives in our Scriptures, for we hear conflicting messages: On one occasion in which Jesus and the disciples were walking, they saw a man who had been born blind. The disciples want to know who sinned, "this man or his parents, that he was born blind?" (John 9:2ff). They remembered the ancient teaching that God punishes children for the sins of their ancestors (Exodus 20:5). Jesus tells them, "Neither one"; yet, healing and forgiveness of sins are paired in several healing narratives. Was Jesus attending to a traditional understanding that suffering results from sin—even though he had denied it in the John 9 account?

> Read these portions of Scripture that connect healing with sin and forgiveness: Luke 5:17-26; John 5:1-14; James 5:13-16. How do you understand them? Consult a study Bible like *The New Interpreter's Study Bible* to see what the study helps suggest. Identify any times in your life where you experienced a connection between healing and forgiveness.

I wonder if suffering and guilt are always so intertwined that I must hear a word of forgiveness if I am to know healing of my whole self. Even if my reason tells me that I am not responsible for my son's death, Jesus knows that healing will only come if I experience the grace that he pours upon that guilty place deep within me. Through forgiveness, Jesus will create the right relationship with us that is the grounding for all healing.

I cannot want or seek healing as long as I am convinced my suffering brings me closer to Jesus. It is hard for me to move toward healing when my deep guilt makes me feel I deserve my suffering. I have found that Julian and others can help free me from the confusing messages about exalting suffering and the links between suffering and guilt—so that I may receive the healing our Kind Mother Jesus has for me.

Redemptive Resurrection Out of Suffering

Julian's words help, but they do not end my dilemmas about suffering and healing. What makes it all very confusing for me—and perhaps you feel it too—is that God creates redemptive resurrections out of suffering. Scripture is filled with a history in which God works through suffering to bring good results. The seed dies, and out of that death comes much fruit. In the face of death, God brings life. That is God's promise. That is also my experience.

> Read Romans 8:28 in the NRSV. Compare the alternative translations in the footnote. Discuss the differences in these translations.

Many of us can understand another of Samuel Miller's prayers:

[W]e thank thee for all those things that seem at first not at all like blessings. . . .[21]

Each of us has stories: a loss of the job you loved—and then a new position that offered opportunities you could not imagine would be yours; the end of a relationship—and then love beyond what you thought possible.

We thank [God] for all those things which seem at first not at all like blessings, yet in which [God's] grace doth manifest its work beyond our understanding.[22]

Some wounds will never entirely heal. Many we cannot ever call blessings. There are wounds and scars that will always ache. We all come with our past, even the worst of it; but nothing— not even the hardest parts—need be lost or wasted.[23] There is strength that comes with those wounds that never completely heal. The most gifted healer may be the wounded one, for many know the truth of Nietzsche's words, "What fails to kill me only makes me stronger." The late theologian Henri Nouwen wrote a book many years ago called *The Wounded Healer* and offered insightful cautions related to both the wounding and the healing.[24]

> Identify experiences—in your own life or in the lives of others—that seemed at first not at all like blessings. In what ways did you experience God's grace working through them?

For some, suffering did not bring strength, but awful bitterness, a kind of death. You know those whose wounds are so deep that they bring more wounding to others than healing. You have those times in your own life when you are immobilized by your suffering. The possibility that good fruit and new life could come out of it is beyond imagining.

What Makes the Difference?

All that we have been exploring about divine healing, and what we will address in succeeding chapters, are part of what makes the difference—God brings good through the blessings of sisters and brothers in Christ, through prayer, through worship and ritual. The naming and recognizing of our suffering has to happen before we can move toward healing and draw strength from our suffering. Ignoring or denying it will only cause delay and more suffering.

Most of us do not desire to make a career of pain. We do not want to dwell always amid scars. To deny our wounds is to miss the blessing God is creating out of our hardest times. To ignore our brokenness denies the miracles God can work to bring new life. God does not want suffering for us. God does not send suffering to punish us or *so that* something good will happen. We know that suffering does find us. And it is God in Christ who stands with us, to strengthen us so that we may—in some mysterious way—wrestle a blessing out of our suffering. The distinctions are critical. They are the difference between life and death.

Closing

Sing two or three times in closing: "Come and Fill Our Hearts." Then join in these prayers:

O God, . . . take the chaos and confusion and disorder of our minds and spirits and hold them so completely in Thy grasp that the impure thing will become pure, . . . and the crass and hard thing will be gentled by Thy spirit. . . . Amen.[25]

—Howard Thurman

*And, Lord, never let me sleep until
I have stretched my hands over my village
and invoked your blessings on it. . . . Amen.*[26]

—Michel Bouttier

Notes

1. "Come and Fill Our Hearts" can be found in *The Faith We Sing* (Nashville: Abingdon Press, 2000), number 2157.

2. Samuel H. Miller, *Prayers for Daily Use* (New York: Harper & Brothers Publishers, 1957), page 90. Your group may prefer to use this adaptation:
Center us down, O God, until in our deepest soul we kneel, quietly, waitfully, reverently. Deliver us from the world for these brief moments, so that we may meet [you] undistractedly, and confirm the bond that binds us to [you]. Then in [your] presence help us to reorder our minds and hearts, bringing before[you] one by one our loved ones, our hopes and fears, our great joys and our ill-admitted sins, until we see with [your] eyes and love with [your] grace.

3. Rita Nakashima Brock and Rebecca Ann Parker, *Proverbs of Ashes: Violence, Redemptive Suffering, and the Search for What Saves Us* (Boston: Beacon Press, 2001).

4. Samuel H. Miller, *The Life of the Soul* (New York: Harper & Row, 1951), page 117.

5. *Julian of Norwich: Showings*, trans. and intro. by Edmund Colledge and James Walsh; preface by Jean Leclercq (New York: Paulist Press, 1978), page 302.

6. *Proverbs of Ashes*, page 18.

7. *Proverbs of Ashes*, page 19.

8. *Proverbs of Ashes*, page 21.

9. *Proverbs of Ashes*, page 21.

10. *Proverbs of Ashes*, page 23.

11. *Proverbs of Ashes*, pages 24–25.

12. *Julian of Norwich*, pages 127–28.

13. *The United Methodist Hymnal* (Nashville: The United Methodist Publishing House, 1997); numbers 421, 535, 424.

14. Emilie M. Townes, ed., *A Troubling in My Soul: Womanist Perspectives on Evil and Suffering* (Maryknoll, NY: Orbis Books, 2001), pages 84, 85, 90.

15. Jane McAvoy, *The Satisfied Life: Medieval Women Mystics on Atonement* (Cleveland, OH: The Pilgrim Press, 2000), page 22.

16. Jane McAvoy, *Communion with the Friends of God: Meditations and Prayers from Women Mystics* (St. Louis: Chalice Press, 2001).

17. *The Satisfied Life*, pages 18–23.

18. *Julian of Norwich*, pages 301–302.

19. Carey Kinsolving and Friends, *Kids Talk About God* (China: J. Countryman, 2001), pages 76–77.

20. Ursula Hegi, *The Vision of Emma Blau* (New York: Simon and Schuster, 2000), page 267.

21. Samuel H. Miller, *Prayers for Daily Use* (New York: Harper and Brothers Publishers, 1957), page 119.

22. *Prayers for Daily Use,* page 119.

23. Roberta C. Bondi, *To Pray and to Love: Conversations on Prayer with the Early Church* (Minneapolis: Fortress Press, 1991), page 135.

24. Henri J. M. Nouwen, *The Wounded Healer: Ministry in Contemporary Society* (Garden City, NY: Doubleday, 1972).

25. Howard Thurman, *The Centering Moment* (New York: Harper & Row, 1969), page 112.

26. Michel Bouttier, *Prayers for My Village* (Nashville: Upper Room Books, 1994), page 58.

CHAPTER 6
"... YOU ANOINT MY HEAD WITH OIL"

How do we experience divine healing through rituals, spiritual practices, and worship?

Focus: This chapter explores the integration of theology, spiritual practices, and divine healing of physical, emotional, and spiritual illness. It looks at the variety of healing worship experiences and how such worship can help people experience divine healing. It also looks at the practices of laying on hands, anointing, and confession and helpful ways they might be used to experience divine healing.

Gathering

Sing together two or three times "Come and Fill Our Hearts."[1] Then join together in prayer:

Center us down, O God, until in our deepest soul we kneel, quietly, waitfully, reverently. Deliver us from the world for these brief moments, so that we may meet thee undistractedly, and confirm the bond that binds us to thee. Then in thy presence help us to reorder our minds and hearts, bringing before thee one by one our loved ones, our hopes and fears, our great joys and our ill-admitted sins, until we see with thine eyes and love with thy grace. [2]

After a few moments of silence, lift concerns for healing that are on your hearts. All respond in prayer: *We bring this care before you.*

Close with these words: *Help us to reorder our minds and hearts, until we see with your eyes and love with your grace. Amen.*

Physical Therapy, Theology, and Spiritual Practice

Have you ever heard of CRPS? I had not, and neither had my former colleague Kathleen. CRPS is Complex Regional Pain Syndrome, an agonizing condition that affects an extremity—a foot or hand. Its cause is unknown, but it often follows some trauma or injury, sometimes as simple as tripping over a shoe. There is a list of clinical symptoms, but they are bland next to Kathleen's own words.

What's the pain like? Like a thousand tiny paper cuts, never cleansed, reopening with every step. Like scrubbing the kitchen floor and ammonia spills onto an open wound. Like a Kansas City hail storm raging through my foot. Like my daughter's rock tumbler, ever grinding grit against jagged pebbles inside my foot, never polished and never smooth.

And what are the feelings? Fear. Fear of the pain itself. Fear of each new therapy exercise that hurts before it heals. Fear it won't get well.[3]

A recent e-mail from Kathleen, to several family members and friends, signaled a victory:

Well, I did it! I graduated today from 16 months of physical therapy work. Way cool!

"Way cool!" did not sound like the studious, meticulous, proper, and sometimes reticent student and colleague I remembered. Kathleen told me that the expression "Way cool!" was for her "joy of months of intense work done well." She knew healing.

How did healing happen? She takes issue with the method taught to doctors and therapists for dealing with CRPS, for it addresses only the disciplines of medicine, psychology, and physiotherapy; that method leaves out the resources of theology and spiritual formation. She does not negate the contributions of the former disciplines. Her appreciation for her therapists is extraordinary; medication made it possible for her to move forward; the support and encouragement of family and friends was invaluable. She describes the significant emotional support she received also from her physical therapists, although she was aware that they often felt "boundary lines" between what they do versus what doctors and counselors do.

80

For Kathleen, theology and spiritual practices combined to become essential elements for her healing. Theology or how one thinks about God *and* spiritual practices or the things a person does to become aware of God's presence were not separate for Kathleen. She lived the practices in the context of her theology; and her theology took form in the practices. For her, these two could not be separated.

How do you think a person's view of God might affect the healing process? What is your view of God? What spiritual practices help you become more aware of God's healing presence?

This insight recalled for me a chaplain who led healing services at a local hospital at a time when such services were unusual. Before he began the service, he framed it in a theology of healing, and he did it with great care. Similarly, an introduction to several liturgies of healing in *The United Methodist Book of Worship* provides a brief but significant discussion of healing from biblical, theological and historical perspectives.

What do you think of the assertion that the rituals or the persons leading them do not do the healing? What does it mean to you to say that such rituals are not magic but they do offer mystery? What roles do you think ritual or spiritual practices play in divine healing?

These theological frameworks offer the grounding for practices and rituals. They make clear that God is the source of healing. We may understand what that means in different ways, but the rituals or practices themselves, and the persons leading them, do not do the healing. This is not magic, though it is indeed mystery.[4]

Kathleen integrated theology and spiritual practice with her physical therapy. For her, as for me, the writings of Joan Chittister on "hope" provided a critical theological resource and the framework for the spiritual practices Kathleen found integral to her healing.

For Further Reading
Read the book *The Psalms: Meditations for Every Day of the Year*. In this book, Sister Joan Chittister has written a series of meditations based on Psalms, offering short readings for each day, based on one psalm each month. In a recent book, she expands upon the theme of struggle and hope, *Scarred by Struggle, Transformed by Hope*.[5]

The problem is that we always think of hope as grounded in the future. Wrong. Hope is always grounded in the past. Hope simply challenges us to remember, always, that we have survived everything in life to this point. . . . [6]

Kathleen had discovered that the practice of "imaging" her foot healed did not work for her. As she heard Chittister's perspective on hope, she realized that imaging was not a practice congruent with her theological grounding. Kathleen saw that the truth Chittister spoke had long been within her heart. It was in the old hymn we had both grown up singing:

Through many dangers, toils and snares,
I have already come;
'tis grace hath brought me safe thus far,
and grace will lead me home.[7]

Kathleen could now name the theological grounding she needed for the next steps of her healing, and she could develop practices congruent with it. She began practices of meditation and journaling in which she recalled all the ways she had come through hard times in the past. She could recall the stories from Scripture and tradition that witnessed to God's repeated activity of healing and salvation in the face of pain and disaster. She knew hope. It was hope rooted in her past and in the past of the people of faith of which she is a part. Hope made her get up in the morning and face into the pain. Hope kept her moving. Hope saved the use of her foot.

Hope led her to music, for she knew the significance of music in her life of faith in the past. The physical therapy method that worked most successfully for her depended upon doing a given number of repetitions of each exercise; but, she says, "I hate to count." She chose a hymn that would last the length of time for the required repetitions. It made the time pass more quickly, and it also had the effect of reinforcing the witness of hope and grace, God's strength and presence. Later, she found she could use the pedal on the piano and each evening played and sang the songs of protest, lament, and hope from *Songs of Zion*.[8] She returned to playing the guitar,

> What spiritual practices similar to those employed by Kathleen do you think might be integrated with medical treatments? What are some experiences that you have had or that you know about in which spiritual and medical practices were combined in a healing process?

and the pain in her tender fingers became a distraction from the agony of her painful foot. Finally, she discovered that when she was singing and playing, her mind did not have room for her pain.

Kathleen found swimming to be another part of her healing and combined her exercise with the practice of the breath prayer.[9]

> The pool was the only place in my waking hours that I could move without pain. And so I began swimming three to six days a week, twenty to twenty-four lengths of the pool each day. With each stroke, I pray a breath prayer: "Lord Jesus, free me from all fear. Grant me thy courage and peace." Each phrase lasts the four to six strokes I need before coming up for air.[10]

Healing and Corporate Spiritual Practice

Kathleen also described corporate practices critical to her healing. A Companions in Christ study group provided both spiritual formation and communal support.

As Kathleen described corporate worship in her local congregation as invaluable in her healing, I reflected upon my experience after our son's death. Our family had been worshiping for several years in a predominantly African American church. The pastoral staff and many of the congregational leaders were colleagues with whom we had worked in the church and community, and we shared their vision and values. We had always been nourished by the worship with its stirring anthems and prophetic preaching. And then Mark died. We returned to worship four days after his memorial service. Never had the worship spoken to us as it did that day, and every Sunday to come.

We were surrounded by a community of survivors, by a culture that knew what suffering meant. Every song, every prayer, every sermon took us first to the depths of pain and

> **For More Information**
> *Companions in Christ* is a program of spiritual formation through small groups. All resources in the series explore classic spiritual practices and invite participants to develop daily patterns that open their lives to a deepening relationship with God and one another. This program, developed by the Board of Discipleship of The United Methodist Church, includes resources prepared by persons from a wide range of theological perspectives. See their Web site at *www.upperroom.org/companions.*

How do you think public worship can be a part of the process of divine healing?

hardship, but refused to leave us there. The power of proclamation, said the dean of African American preachers, Gardner Taylor, "is in a heart broken, and put together, by the eternal God."[11] We were blessed to be with a community who recognized suffering, whose beginnings were shaped by the terrors of history, who had walked many trails of tears, and who were not afraid to weep. We could go and unashamedly take our suffering with us. Because we were able to do that, we could begin to heal, a very small piece at a time.

By contrast, I remember a New England minister who preached a Thanksgiving Eve service in 1963 without naming the assassination of President Kennedy five days before and the anguish we felt. I remember hearing one who is dear to me talk of the prophetic sermons her pastor preached each week during the years of Vietnam, but she could not hear a word for her pain or her husband's

How do you think worship and ritual can be "wounding" for those who need healing?

as his cancer was destroying his body. I think of services I have planned and led where there was no welcoming space for the broken-hearted.

Every experience of worship and ritual can be healing or wounding. A sense of isolation is one of the most damaging dimensions of illness, grief, or any form of hardship. Those who come with their suffering, and find in worship no resonance for it, may leave with more pain in their hearts and less trust in the church.

For More Information
Read *Standing in the Circle of Grief,* by Blair Gilmer Meeks (Abingdon Press, 2002). The prayers, Scripture lessons, and other contributions in this volume sensitively, and with theological acumen, address loss in multiple forms, from the beginning moments, through anniversary and holiday seasons, and in ordinary time. While composed to be used by congregations, these carefully crafted pieces of liturgy provide rich resources for individuals or parts of the congregation to use as well.

In the title of her recent book, Blair Gilmer Meeks has affirmed our need to have others stand with us. *Standing in the Circle of Grief* includes prayers for use throughout the church year that take into account those who know loss.[12]

I am often puzzled by those who worry lest the mention of a loss or a hardship "stir up the old pain" or "make you feel worse." Do they think that somehow I forget, for a moment, that my son has died? Do they believe that my friend did not remember he had AIDS until someone spoke the word? Our sisters and brothers in Christ depend upon us to be there and not to look away. Some will choose to be more private than others, and few want to be defined by our hardships. But a word of care is seldom unwelcome. That care can be expressed in worship by the choice of words in a prayer, or in a

For Further Information
Among the finest resources for liturgy related to HIV/AIDS is the program Balm in Gilead (*www.balmingilead.org*). One collection of prayers and other resources for worship is appropriately titled *Who Will Break the Silence? Liturgical Resources for The Healing of AIDS* (copyright © 1995 The Balm in Gilead, Inc.). It was prepared for the 2nd Annual Black Church National Day of Prayer for the Healing of AIDS. Congregations from many different traditions will find this a valuable resource.[13]

generalized concern (if the hardship or illness is not known by all). It can be shown by a touch of care during the passing of the peace or following a service. Any one of us, lay and clergy, can help make ritual and worship a time of healing.

Such acknowledgment becomes even more critical when suffering is in the category of disenfranchised grief or hardships that some choose not to name. Disenfranchised grief is experienced when we incur loss that cannot be openly acknowledged, socially supported, or publicly mourned. This kind of grief and hardship is often experienced, for example, by persons in gay or lesbian relationships or in other partnerships that are not "official." Some persons experience substantial grief when they lose a pet, but that is seldom a socially supported grief.

The congregation where we were worshiping developed a ministry with persons affected by HIV/AIDS and their families, a group whose grief has been disenfranchised in many of our communities. Several times each year, this group prepared the liturgy for worship—naming the congregation's covenant to care for those some churches did not welcome.

Healing Services

While any service of worship can be wounding or healing, in recent years there has been renewed interest in worship particularly designed as healing services. United Methodists, for example, can find in *The United Methodist Book of Worship*[14] an entire section entitled "Healing Services and Prayers." If one compares earlier worship resources, it becomes clear that the place of healing in the life of the church and our corporate worship has shifted significantly in the past thirty years.

This current worship resource stands in contrast to the denomination's previous *Book of Worship,* published in 1964, which contained no services of healing (although there is "An Office for the Dedication of a Hospital," page 365). The prayers "For the Sick and Sorrowing" were in the section "General Prayers," which also included table graces and a form for family prayer. While portions of this collection could have been included in congregational worship, it was separate from the section called "For Use in Corporate Worship."

As I have worked with these services, I have grown in my appreciation for the care with which they were composed and the breadth of situations they address. The inclusion of a section on "Ministry with Persons Going Through Divorce" is itself ministry for those who often feel isolated and unwelcome during a time filled, at the least, with uncertainty and, often, with brokenness and anger and hurt. "A Service of Hope after Loss of Pregnancy" brings to light the sorrow many families have hidden through the years. The lists of Scripture passages and hymns throughout this section of the *Book of Worship* testify to the wealth of perspectives and approaches that healing may take.

> Attend a healing service. Give attention to what you see to be the theological groundings for healing in this service.

> What images first come to your mind when you hear "healing service"? "laying on of hands"? "faith healing"? What are the pictures in your mind? How do these images express God's healing presence? How might they suggest "magic?"

Earlier I spoke of the careful introduction to these services. Here are the cautions that remind us that all healing is of God, and the services do not offer magic. Healing is not the same as curing. The disclaimers are here. And why must that be? Why does it seem necessary to spend more effort clarifying what "healing services" are *not* than testifying to God's wondrous presence in our lives in the midst of suffering?

For many of us, the images of healing services come from television's flamboyant purveyors of "miracle healings"; and those experiences tend to raise questions. We read of frauds and misrepresentations. We know that large amounts of money are involved, and it is hard not to be suspicious of motives.

How, then, are we to think of healing services? Some avoid leading or attending because they consider such services to be a misuse or misunderstanding of Christian healing in popular culture. Healing services take many forms in order that many people, who have many ways of expressing faith in God, may relate to the God who desires healing and wholeness. Some need the formality of liturgy and written word. Others need movement and freedom for individual expression. God's healing presence is not limited by particular ways of worshiping. Pentecostal worship services, prayer services that are more informal and spontaneous, formal services that rely heavily upon written liturgy, and all services in which people trust in God's healing presence will hold the potential for participants to experience the healing power of God.

> Watch a healing service on television, such as those led by Benny Hinn. Identify what you see to be the theological grounding for these popular faith healers. Compare to other healing services you have attended. Compare to your own theological understanding of healing, that is, to the way you think God is at work in the healing process.

I find it helpful to look at our call to participate in healing services as simple faithfulness. I pray each day—not because I understand how prayer "works" and often in spite of the ways in which I observe prayer being misused around me. I pray because Scripture is full of admonitions to pray. And I partake of the Lord's Supper each time it is offered, not because I understand, but because Jesus called me to do it, in remembrance of him. Are there any among us who are ill? What are we called to do? to gather and pray over them. (Read James 5:14-16 for the instructions the early church received.). Such prayer expresses simple faithfulness grounded in hope. Through the centuries, the people of God have gathered and prayed over sisters and brothers who were sick, who were broken in heart and spirit. They witness to healing. It was not always the healing for which they asked. They may not have experienced a "cure." But, they tell us, they were bonded with the One who is the Healer and often received more than they could ask or imagine.

The Healing Potential of Confession, Repentance, and Reconciliation

Some kinds of brokenness require additional consideration. The student who lives with the memories of abuse by her brother many years ago cries out for healing. The distortions in our culture have placed within her a skewed sense of responsibility and guilt and shame for what someone else did. What is healing for her?

The young Richard Wright writes of shame as he leaves a "boxing match" into which he and a friend had been manipulated as entertainment for the white men where they worked.

> I heard of other fights being staged between other black boys, and each time I heard those plans falling from the lips of the white men in the factory I eased out of earshot. I felt that I had done something unclean, something for which I could never properly atone.[15]

In some traditions, what was once called *penance* now is the sacrament or act of *reconciliation*. The one who has wronged another makes a confession and may receive counsel, then absolution, and a prayer of thanksgiving follows.

But what of the one who has been wronged? What of the one who is not guilty but feels guilt and shame? What of ones upon whom guilt and shame weigh so heavily they cannot speak their anguish? Howard Thurman, in a meditation entitled "Rekindle Our Memories," suggests a starting point. Amid a long list of persons and situations "we remember," he writes:

> We remember those from whom have come to us the things that hurt, that wound, that bruise, that create anguish.

He then prays to God before whom we spread "the entire panoply of our lives, the things that we affect and the things that affect us."

> And we seek to find a way to look at them, a way to feel about them, that is in accordance with Thy will and Thy purpose and Thy concern.[16]

Could it be that I can look at an abuser with anger and cry out for his contrition and penance—and still be in accordance with God's will and purpose and concern? Roberta Bondi's work on the desert fathers and mothers adds that when we pray for others, "Wanting another's well-being is not necessarily wanting what he or she wants."[17] And Marjorie Suchocki discovered what she calls John Wesley's "rather amazing instruction that we should confess the sins of others as our own"[18]:

> We ought . . . to bear the defects of others and our own, to confess them to God in secret prayer.[19]

What kind of ritual can address the anguished woman who *feels* her shame must be cleansed—when another is responsible? What can bring a just healing for the one who has been wronged by the racial sickness within and outside him—when he feels it is he who must atone?

Jan Richardson, a United Methodist clergywoman and artist, was invited by a friend to prepare a prayer of confession for a ritual of healing from abuse. She writes of her belief that "at the heart of confession lies the power to name: not simply to name what we have done wrong but to name what has been done to us and to name our own struggles to claim responsibility for our healing."[20] Her confession, then, speaks to the God of compassion:

> Talk together about this dilemma. What kind of ritual might there be? What would you include in it?

> we acknowledge the times
> we have lived too long . . .
> with the pain [others] have written
> onto our bodies, . . .
> with the shame they have inscribed
> onto our souls.[21]

Some think of rituals as ancient things, but ritual making is an on-going process. Each day, we develop new rituals for healing, and we do it with attention to the context and the needs of the ones seeking healing.

The Laying On of Hands

The laying on of hands has been an important part of healing rituals for centuries. What is the power of touch? I read often of studies that indicate tiny babies thrive when they know the warmth of touch. I remember an older woman who came to seminary several years after her husband had died. As we did an exercise in orientation that involved laying hands on one another's shoulders, she wept quietly. "It has been so long since someone has touched me," she said. "I did not know how much I ached for it."

But what of the anguished woman for whom touch was abuse? What of others for whom touch is frightening? What one intends as a gentle embrace of care in the passing of the peace, another may find alarming. How do we know?

> What kinds of touch are "safe" and healing? Do you find some kinds of touch hurtful? How do you communicate to another what is acceptable to you? How do you learn from someone else what could be healing and what could be hurtful?

As the familiar psalm reminds us, anointing with oil has long been a holy sign of healing (Psalm 23:5b). During Advent, I planned for our still grieving congregation a service of "light and healing." We acknowledged together how hard this time is for those of us who know grief, illness, or hardship. As Nicholas Wolterstorff writes, "The gap is too great between day and heart."[22] As I received the touch of oil on my forehead, and then touched others with the oil as they came forward, I grew aware both of how significant that touch was and also how "safe" it felt. This very ritualized form of touch may be an important place to start in services of healing.

These questions of safe touch suggest one among many reasons our rituals of healing are best done within the context of an on-going community of faith—among persons who have familiarity with one another and are committed to learning about one another. Within the Christian tradition, healing is connected with relationships—our relationship

> Read James 5:13-16. What insights do you gain about divine healing from this Scripture? What connections do you make between forgiveness of sin and healing? How do you think this Scripture might address some of the questions raised about prayer, touch, anointing, forgiveness, and healing?

with the One who promised healing and our relationships with our villages that surround us with care. Our healing rituals and practices and worship—whether lived in the silence of a study or sung in the exercise room or celebrated in the filled sanctuary—are always "ours," not "mine."

Closing
   Sing two or three times in closing: "Come and Fill Our Hearts." Then join in these prayers:

O God, . . . take the chaos and confusion and disorder of our minds and spirits and hold them so completely in Thy grasp that the impure thing will become pure, . . . and the crass and hard thing will be gentled by Thy spirit. . . . Amen. [23]
   —Howard Thurman

*And, Lord, never let me sleep until
I have stretched my hands over my village
and invoked your blessings on it. . . . Amen.*[24]
   —Michel Bouttier

NOTES

   1. "Come and Fill Our Hearts" can be found in *The Faith We Sing* (Nashville: Abingdon Press, 2000), number 2157.
   2. Samuel H. Miller, *Prayers for Daily Use* (New York: Harper & Brothers Publishers, 1957), page 90. Your group may prefer to pray this adaptation: *Center us down, O God, until in our deepest soul we kneel, quietly, waitfully, reverently. Deliver us from the world for these brief moments, so that we may meet [you] undistractedly, and confirm the bond that binds us to [you]. Then in [your] presence help us to reorder our minds and hearts, bringing before[you] one by one our loved ones, our hopes and fears, our great joys and our ill-admitted sins, until we see with [your] eyes and love with [your] grace.*
   3. Kathleen Campbell, Unpublished writings. Kathleen would welcome conversation with others who experience the challenges of CRPS or other chronic pain conditions. E-mail Kathleen at *kcampbell@ups.edu*.
   4. *The United Methodist Book of Worship* (Nashville: The United Methodist Publishing House, 1993), pages 613–14.
   5. Joan Chittister, *Scarred by Struggle, Transformed by Hope* (Grand Rapids, MI.: William B. Eerdmans Publishing, 2003).
   6. Joan Chittister, *The Psalms: Meditations for Every Day of the Year* (New York: The Crossroad Publishing Company, 1996), page 50.
   7. "Amazing Grace," *The United Methodist Hymnal* (Nashville: The United Methodist Publishing House, 1997), number 378.
   8. *Songs of Zion* (Nashville: Abingdon Press, 1984).
   9. A breath prayer is described by Ron DelBene in *The Breath of Life: A*

Simple Way to Pray (Nashville, TN: The Upper Room, 1996). It's a prayer of six to eight syllables that flows smoothly when spoken aloud or expressed as a heart thought. It includes *a name to call God* (such as Jesus, Shepherd, Eternal Light) and *a request for what I want* (such as peace, love, rest, guidance).

10. Kathleen Campbell, unpublished writings.

11. Gardner Taylor, "A Wide Vision Through a Narrow Window," Quoted in Michael Eric Dyson, *Christian Century*, "Gardner Taylor: Poet Laureate of the Pulpit" (January 4-11, 1995), page 16.

12. Blair Gilmer Meeks, *Standing in the Circle of Grief: Prayers and Liturgies for Death and Dying* (Nashville: Abingdon Press, 2002).

13. *Who Will Break the Silence? Liturgical Resources for the Healing of AIDS* (New York: The Balm in Gilead, Inc., 1995).

14. *The United Methodist Book of Worship*, pages 613–29.

15. Richard Wright, *Black Boy: A Record of Childhood and Youth* (New York: Harper & Row, 1945), page 266.

16. Howard Thurman, *The Centering Moment* (New York: Harper & Row, 1969), page 64.

17. Roberta C. Bondi, *To Pray and to Love: Conversations on Prayer with the Early Church* (Minneapolis: Fortress Press, 1991), page 114.

18. Marjorie Suchocki, "The Perfection of Prayer," in Randy L. Maddox, ed., *Rethinking Wesley's Theology for Contemporary Methodism* (Nashville: Abingdon Press, 1998), page 52.

19. John Wesley, *A Plain Account of Christian Perfection*, ¶25, Q. 38, §2, *Works* (Jackson) 11:436.

20. Jan L. Richardson, *In Wisdom's Path: Discovering the Sacred in Every Season* (Cleveland, OH: The Pilgrim Press, 2000), page 82.

21. *In Wisdom's Path,* page 82.

22. Nicholas Wolterstorff, *Lament for a Son* (Grand Rapids, MI: William B. Eerdmans Publishing, 1987), page 61.

23. Howard Thurman, *The Centering Moment* (New York: Harper & Row, 1969), page 112.

24. Michel Bouttier, *Prayers for My Village* (Nashville: Upper Room Books, 1994), page 58.

CHAPTER 7
"WHETHER WE LIVE OR WHETHER WE DIE, WE ARE THE LORD'S"

What can healing mean in the face of death?

Focus: This chapter explores how divine healing may be experienced when death seems imminent. It looks at a variety of ways that becoming whole is experienced as divine healing. In addition, it raises questions surrounding quality of life, extraordinary measures for prolonging life, and how some have viewed death itself as healing.

Gathering

Sing together two or three times "Come and Fill Our Hearts."[1] Then join together in prayer:

Center us down, O God, until in our deepest soul we kneel, quietly, waitfully, reverently. Deliver us from the world for these brief moments, so that we may meet thee undistractedly, and confirm the bond that binds us to thee. Then in thy presence help us to reorder our minds and hearts, bringing before thee one by one our loved ones, our hopes and fears, our great joys and our ill-admitted sins, until we see with thine eyes and love with thy grace.[2]

After a few moments of silence, lift concerns for healing that are on your hearts. All respond in prayer: *We bring this care before you.*

Close with these words: *Help us to reorder our minds and hearts, until we see with your eyes and love with your grace. Amen.*

Linda's Journal

Everyone listens to your pain for a while,
some out of curiosity,
some thankful that it is not their pain,
some relieved that you are not so strong after all.
But even friends grow weary of hearing the same old pain.
So do the curious and the compassionate.
Finally, we end up talking silently to ourselves.
Maybe the healing takes place when even *we* are bored [italics added].[3]

Thus begins a series of journal entries written by a woman who was preparing to die.

Healing doesn't necessarily mean physical recovery. I may not get well. But healing can mean becoming whole before you die. . . . I simply can't remain the same person who got sick.[4]

Linda has known suffering and healing, grief and renewed life. Years before, she lost one she loved in a faraway, confusing war. At the close of the war, she traveled to that distant land to help lead frightened families to a place of safety. Some were not saved; she describes lifeblood flowing into the street as she watched. She chose to live her life in the face of that experience of deaths. She lived fully, offering her gifts of exceptional intelligence, determination, and honed skills, first in one field of service and then in another. She would have been happy as a perennial student, but she knew she was gifted to serve. Then she became ill. Her family was familiar with illness; her sister had lived with disease much of her life. Now Linda had a brain tumor.

> Do you know persons whose illness has taken them to the edge of life? Talk with them if they are willing. How did they experience that time? Did they have an understanding of what healing might mean when they had no assurance that physical healing was possible?

Raw Fear and Unrelenting Hope

Linda used her gift for crafting words as a companion in her time of anguish. She had moments of hope that lived beside her suffering:

I am feeling better. It is almost miraculous.

I have spent the better part of the last year submerged in unrelenting pain. Pain, and this disease have swept a million dreams into the ocean. Fighting it has robbed me of gusto and even small pleasures, eroding my sense of the sacred and meaningful in life.

The healing is fragile, I know, incomplete and temporary, but quite real. I have begun to feel an interior strength flicker to life, my body gaining power, my soul once again feeling God's touch. I am back in business again.

But not long after, the business appeared to close.

There are still times when I think myself to be a failure because my body is so obviously deteriorating, despite all my efforts to heal myself within and without.

I'm trying to understand the process of healing taking place within the process of my dying. The goal now is a deep serenity, peace of mind—perfect balance, a relaxed body and a rich, hearty soul.

Linda's journal continues with the poetic descriptions and insights that capture her "raw fear and unrelenting hope," so that her heart swells "with sorrow and joy in equal, unbearable measure." She witnesses to the ways God has given her prayer. She returns to the experience of wonder, for "wonder is almost always possible." Yet she confesses to feeling battle-worn. "It's hard to describe how utterly dark the world can look at times." Finally, in the last selections from her journal that I have, she writes,

Part of me still sees this as a battle for my life. But now it's a special sort of battle. Not a battle defined by aggression or competition. But a battle defined by honor, compassion, and grace. A battle where there is no failure, only healing and becoming whole.

It is eleven years later. Linda's sister has died. Linda survives.

Linda grieves anew and also lives that special kind of battle, continually, defined by "honor, compassion and grace . . . where there is no failure, only healing and becoming whole." Buried in her journal was Linda's reminder to herself that her admonitions about living in the face of death described "the way I want to live out my life, regardless of the progress of the disease."

> When have you known both "raw fear and unrelenting hope?" What does Linda's struggle say to you about divine healing? about God? about fear? about hope?

Linda's journal entries are a treasure for me, for they are not the remembering of one who has recovered physically from an illness and looks back on what it was like. These are the cries of lament and psalms of hope from the edge of life. Here was one who grew clear about the healing required of her in the light of her body's deterioration.

> What does "not remaining the same person who became ill" suggest to you?

. . . [H]ealing can mean becoming whole before you die. . . . I simply can't remain the same person who got sick.

Becoming whole? Not remaining the same person who became ill? What can that mean?

"So Short a Time to Learn So Much?"

At the beginning of her short novel *I Heard the Owl Call My Name*, Margaret Craven records a conversation between a bishop and a doctor regarding Mark, a young priest. The doctor reports that the priest has only two "active years" before illness will weaken him and then take his life. And the bishop responds, "So short a time to learn so much?"[5]

Two years later, the bishop has returned to the Alaskan Indian village to which he had sent Mark. It is the place the bishop then describes:

> . . . [I]t has always been easier here, where only the fundamentals count, to learn what every [one] must learn in this world. . . .
> Enough of the meaning of life to be ready to die.[6]

What did that mean for Mark?

> Here, where death waited behind each tree, he had made friends with loneliness, with death and deprivation, and, solidly against his back had stood the wall of his faith. . . .

[W]hat had he learned? . . . He had seen the sadness, the richness, the tragic poignancy of a way of life that each year, bit by bit, slipped beyond memory and was gone. For a time he had been part of it, one of the small unknown men who take their stand in some remote place, and fight out their battle in a quiet way.[7]

He had suffered with the people, and "now you are theirs, and nothing will ever be the same again."[8]

> If possible, find and read *I Heard the Owl Call My Name,* by Margaret Craven. What insights does it offer to you about finding meaning in the face of death? What do the words "now you are theirs, and nothing will ever be the same again" suggest to you about meaning? What do they suggest about the connections between healing and the feeling of "belonging"? Write several entries for your own journal, entitled "What I want to learn before I die."

Becoming Whole

In Margaret Kim Peterson's writing about her husband's last days (described in Chapter 1), Peterson told of the healing of who her husband was as a person with others and with himself. "[H]e was present and open, able to love and to be loved. . . ." Unlike the gift of Linda's journal, we do not have Hyung Goo's own words about his work of healing in the face of death. We do not know if he was saying, as his wife did, "It was not the sort of healing that we had hoped or asked for. How could we have asked for it, when we couldn't even imagine it?"[9]

Becoming whole. Whatever it looks like, it will be the mystery that God brings—far beyond all we could ask or imagine. For Hyung Goo, it was living present and open, loving and being loved. For Mark, the young priest, it was becoming part—and not part—of a rich and sad way of life; he had befriended death, with the wall of his faith solidly behind. He knew enough to die.

The vision Linda described was "a deep serenity, peace of mind—perfect balance, a relaxed body and a rich, hearty soul." But she also wrote of doing "what you can do today. This moment. . . . [and] understand that you don't know what comes next." So when she came to a place that appeared to be closest to the face of death, she wrote:

These days I approach life with increasing simplicity. Sometimes the accomplishment is nothing more—and nothing less—than simply being here.

What is healing in the face of death? Wholeness. Simplicity. Being here. Present. Open. Loving and being loved. Not the same person who became sick. Befriending death. Not what any would have known to ask or imagine.

> **What does "becoming whole" mean to you?**

Healing for the Bitter and the Alienated

Some of those who are ill grow increasingly unlike the person who became ill; yet the movement is not toward healing but toward bitterness and alienation. For some, it is the result of dementia and confusion. For others, the increasing loss of control is crushing; they strike out in anger. What is healing for them?

Some give up or die in spirit. A hurt or betrayal may be too great to bear. In one of those mystery/detective stories that is about more than the plot, Martha Grimes describes the feeling. Jury, the detective, discovers it is the man he loved and trusted who had slain their friend. Now it was Jury this man was trying to kill.

> In another moment of standing there, . . . Jury felt something leave him. . . . He thought it was hope. And it was gone for good. If he lived, something that looked like it would come back: a poor imitation, a shadow, but not the real thing.[10]

What will healing be—for the bitter and alienated, for the hopeless and the hopelessly confused? Some will not know healing before the death of their bodies, but death itself becomes the healing.

> **For Further Reading:**
> *The Story of My Father* recounts the life and dying of Sue Miller's father, James Nichols, a church historian and retired seminary dean. Her story looks back at what she imagines was the beginning of her father's disease and describes starkly his descent into the shadows of increasing dementia.

The novelist Sue Miller writes of her father and their family's experience of his Alzheimer's disease. She confessed she had "thought death finished a person's story, that it was part of the narrative arc of someone's life and made a kind of final sense of it. . . . I thought you *earned* a certain kind of death."[11] Then she lived through her father's dying. She watched the disease twist his mind. She suffered when she was with him, and she was not pleased with herself when she stayed away.

Miller's father then developed a condition that was immediately life-threatening, and what she felt was *"relief* for Dad. A kind of joy, really."[12]

> That he should die now, that he should die naturally and quickly before he lost completely his sense of who he was, who he'd been, this seemed to me a pure boon, a generous and unexpected gift, the answer to the prayers implicit in the formal, formulaic language of his living will. . . .
> . . . I was glad that my father's body had found the way out, the reprieve from what had been waiting for him.[13]

She confessed to shame and guilt for feeling that way, but she was clear: death was healing.

Nancy Cruzan's family found no such relief for seven years. Nancy Cruzan's body found no way out of the "persistent vegetative state" in which she lived following an automobile accident. For seven years, the family fought bureaucracies and government until the courts gave permission for her to be allowed to die. It was seven years between the death of her awareness and the acknowledged death of her body. William Colby, an attorney who worked with the Cruzan family, entitled his book about this journey of anguish *Long Goodbye: The Deaths of Nancy Cruzan.* Two deaths, with seven years between.[14]

> Have you been close to persons who have become confused through Alzheimer's disease or similar conditions? Compare your response to that of Sue Miller.

It was but seven days that we stood at the bedside of our son. We watched the monitors as they showed less and less motion. We learned that the involuntary movement of his leg through the air was called *posturing*—a word I no longer can use for the pretentious way some people act. "When I hear someone else say it, I see Mark, his leg slightly bent, lifted above the bed. Nothing pretentious. Involuntary. Unconscious. Entirely unconscious."[15] In the middle of our seven-day vigil came the Supreme Court decision that ended the Cruzan family's seven-year watch. At the end of our seven days, the doctor said simply that Mark was dead, brain dead. I share with William Colby and the Cruzan family the agony of a brain death, a real death, but one that is not always called death. It is then that the second death can be healing.

As I write, another young woman lives in consciousness without awareness. Her death of awareness occurred the same year the Supreme Court allowed Nancy Cruzan's family to discontinue the artificial means that were keeping her alive. Thirteen years later, the thirteen years in which I have been learning to love the Mark who no longer lives and breathes beside us, the family of Terri Schiavo still struggles to discover what it means to love Terri. Some parts of the family hold tenaciously to their belief that love means keeping her body alive with a feeding tube. Another part of her family believes that to love is to allow her body to die. A legislature and a governor have become parties to the struggle, and many of us from faraway feel party to it as well. Who has the right to make these decisions? What is in the best interest of this woman? Courts and attorneys become the primary players. Columnists plead with the rest of us to make our wishes known through advance directives. Parents of children with severe disabilities ask the "slippery slope" question.

Many days I give thanks that this set of decisions was not ours to make. What would I do? How would I know what was faithful? How would I decide how best to love Mark? I prayed that if he could not get well, I wanted him to die. But I could not have said then what I meant by "well." Would I only want him to survive if he could be all that he had been before the accident? Could I learn to love a different Mark? How different? Conscious but unaware? In a persistent vegetative state? Yes, I would love him. I love him still. And yet, it is hard for me to imagine choosing that he live without awareness. What is it that determines the quality of life for which I want to be kept alive? How do I decide for one I love? How do I tell one I love how to decide for me?

> Talk about your responses to the debates surrounding Nancy Cruzan and Terri Schiavo. Imagine you are the parent or spouse of one of them.

Extraordinary Measures?

Health and wholeness. Being alive. Surviving. Authentic life. Human life. Dignity. What do these mean when a mind is not at work in any way I can discern? What do these mean when a body has deteriorated beyond repair? More than one columnist and preacher urged us this week to make our decisions about death while we are alive. But first, I must be clear

100

about what it means to be alive in the way I would choose to go on living. I must also hear what it means for those I love—if they are asking me to carry out their directives.

My husband and his best friend had a "routine" they would sometimes rehearse when prompted by circumstances like those being debated now. With deep care for each other and humor that masked the depth of their feelings, they would talk about what would happen when they grew old: They would rock together on the porch "at the home," and they promised each other that they would see that something was done if either of them got too bad. I suspect that what seemed like "too bad" shifted over the years from what they imagined when their friendship started as young men.

When that dear friend was dying several years ago, the story had been told so often that family and friends knew well that he wanted no extraordinary measures to keep him "surviving" beyond what we had come to know was authentic living in his eyes. He had made it clear: when that time came, death would be healing for him.

Columnists and preachers are urging us to make decisions while we are alive, but that makes it sound clear and unambiguous. Such decisions call me to examine, at a depth I might not have before, what determines the quality of life I want sustained and under what conditions I consider death to be healing.

And what is it saying about death if I—or those I love—determine that hanging on to survival, without awareness, is preferable to death? What can it mean for me to witness to the power of resurrection and proclaim, "Whether we live or whether we die, we are the Lord's," and then hold on to a life that looks more like death than living? How do I reflect upon those questions? with whom?

> Consider your own questions. Write an advance directive, or review yours if you have already prepared it. What does it say about the conditions under which you want to be kept alive?

Resurrection

I discovered when Mark died that my theology of resurrection was tested and transformed.

Now [resurrection] has to do with the everlasting life of my son, the resurrection of this body to which I first gave birth. . . . It is my fervent mother-
hope that my baby, my firstborn child, is not lost forever, is not lost *to me*
forever, is not lost.

I used to be amused at questions about what our bodies would be like in the
resurrection—whether we would recognize one another. What did it matter? It matters now.[16]

I believe in resurrection. What that means matters in a way far beyond
what I imagined before. I have few answers; for, as the writer of First John
says, "what we will be has not yet been revealed" (3:2). It is enough to say
with Paul, "Whether we live or whether we die, we are the Lord's"
(Romans 14:8).

I also know a resurrection in this life—a presence that lives beside the
palpable absence. Zora Neale Hurston, through her character Janie (in
Their Eyes Were Watching God), captures the reality of that presence with
incomparable images. Janie's beloved husband, strangely named "Tea
Cake," was dead. As she sat alone in her bedroom, the memories of his
death "commenced to sing a sobbing sigh out of every corner in the room
. . ."

Then Tea Cake came prancing around her where she was and the song of
the sigh flew out of the window and lit in the top of the pine trees. Tea
Cake, with the sun for a shawl. Of course he wasn't dead. He could never
be dead until she herself had finished feeling and thinking. The kiss of his
memory made pictures of love and light against the wall. Here was peace.
. . . She called in her soul to come and see.[17]

Tea Cake is not gone. Mark is not gone.

In *The United Methodist Book of Worship* are prayers that witness to
this presence. I pray adaptations of them often in corporate worship for
memorial services or All Saints Day.

We remember them with gratitude and bless their names. For all they have
given us to make us what we are, for every gift that lives and grows within
us, and for their lives that in your love will never end, we give you thanks.

We give thanks that they now live and reign with you. Fulfill in them your
purpose that reaches beyond time and death. They are alive forevermore.
Amen.

Whether We Live or Whether We Die . . .

What can healing mean in the face of imminent death? Linda was determined not to be the same person who became ill. Mark, the priest, had befriended death, with the wall of his faith at his back. For Nancy Cruzan's family, healing came with her death. I witness to the conviction that healing happens always in relation to the One who is Healer and Savior. "Whether we live or whether we die, we are the Lord's."

What will be my healing in the face of death? During Advent of this year, I came to a new sense of what it might be. In the congregation where I have been in ministry, one Advent/Christmas refrain has become a balm upon broken hearts. It was at the beginning of Advent the year before that the congregation experienced the news that one they loved had brought hurt into their midst. In those first weeks, they ended each service of worship with "Emmanuel, Emmanuel."[18]

Many spoke of the power of the words speaking to their brokenness: "God with us." As we entered a second Advent, we again sang of Emmanuel, God with us. This time, I have become more attentive to another phrase in this short hymn. "God with us" and also "God revealed in us."

What do I hope for my healing in the face of death? As I pray each day with Samuel Miller that our minds and hearts may be reordered, and sing each Sunday of God revealed in us, then healing must mean

living and praying within the community of faith,
until we see with God's eyes and love with God's grace,
and until God is, indeed, revealed in us.

Closing

Sing two or three times in closing: "Come and Fill Our Hearts." Then join in these prayers:

O God, . . . take the chaos and confusion and disorder of our minds and spirits and hold them so completely in Thy grasp that the impure thing will become pure, . . . and the crass and hard thing will be gentled by Thy spirit. . . . Amen.[19]

—Howard Thurman

And, Lord, never let me sleep until
I have stretched my hands over my village
and invoked your blessings on it. . . . Amen.[20]

—Michel Bouttier

Notes

1. "Come and Fill Our Hearts" can be found in *The Faith We Sing* (Nashville: Abingdon Press, 2000), number 2157.

2. Samuel H. Miller, *Prayers for Daily Use* (New York: Harper & Brothers Publishers, 1957), page 90. Your group may prefer to pray this adaptation:
Center us down, O God, until in our deepest soul we kneel, quietly, waitfully, reverently. Deliver us from the world for these brief moments, so that we may meet [you] undistractedly, and confirm the bond that binds us to [you]. Then in [your] presence help us to reorder our minds and hearts, bringing before[you] one by one our loved ones, our hopes and fears, our great joys and our ill-admitted sins, until we see with [your] eyes and love with [your] grace.

3. Linda Brown, unpublished journal.

4. Linda Brown.

5. Margaret Craven, *I Heard the Owl Call My Name* (Garden City, NY: Doubleday & Company, 1973), page 11.

6. *I Heard the Owl Call My Name,* pages 149–50.

7. *I Heard the Owl Call My Name,* page 151.

8. *I Heard the Owl Call My Name,* page 91.

9. Kim Peterson, *Sing Me to Heaven: The Story of a Marriage* (Grand Rapids, MI: Brazos Press, 2003), pages 134–35.

10. Martha Grimes, *The Blue Last: A Richard Jury Mystery* (New York: Viking Press, 2001), page 412.

11. Sue Miller, *The Story of My Father* (New York: Alfred A. Knopf, 2003), page 87.

12. *The Story of My Father,* page 150.

13. *The Story of My Father,* pages 150–51.

14. William H. Colby, *Long Goodbye: The Deaths of Nancy Cruzan* (Carlsbad, CA: Hay House, 2002).

15. Susan Sonnenday Vogel, *And Then Mark Died: Letters of Grief, Love, and Faith* (Nashville: Abingdon Press, 2003), page 78.

16. *And Then Mark Died,* page 17.

17. Zora Neale Hurston, *Their Eyes Were Watching God* (New York: Perennial, 1990), pages 183–84.

18. "Emmanuel, Emmanual," *The United Methodist Hymnal* (Nashville: The United Methodist Publishing House, 1997), number 204.

19. Howard Thurman, *The Centering Moment* (New York: Harper & Row, 1969), page 112.

20. Michel Bouttier, *Prayers for My Village* (Nashville: Upper Room Books, 1994), page 58.

CONCLUDING WORDS

Jane is a breast cancer survivor. Her illness and healing led her back to a call to ministry that had moved in her heart for many years. She is a highly regarded community leader, and her work with and on behalf of children has been recognized with prominent awards. She turned her gifts toward the church and began seminary. What brilliance and good sense she brought to the classroom.

Then one afternoon, she sat in my office and spoke the words: "The cancer is back. It's not good." She and her doctors had agreed to a plan for radical, experimental treatment. It was fall. The chemotherapy would stretch through the winter and into spring.

As she began treatment, Jane gathered her family and friends in her backyard. She asked us to choose flower bulbs from the sacks on the porch, take a shovel, and plant. Through the winter and into spring, she would watch the yard from her window. She called us her bulb-planting angels. When Jane speaks of angels, she does not have in mind the sweet nightgown-clad type. She had studied Scripture well. She understood angels to be powerful creatures, those who had to call, "Fear not," lest the hearers flee in terror. Tough and tenacious angels. Praying and long-suffering angels.

Jane gathered us around her, and as we planted, there was the healing born of long and faithful friendships; a sense of right relationship was confirmed among those who loved her. She knew that God was working in and through the gifts and graces of the community she called her bulb-planting angels.

Winter came. It was long. She sat by her window and watched the snow-covered yard. God did bring spring that year, and Jane brought her bulb-planting angels back together.

The seeds of friendship blossom in the soul.

Angels are invited to appear at any time between 1:00 p.m. and 5:00 p.m. and to hover around the flowers as long as they wish.

Bulb-planting angels are mortal embodiments of loving cosmic forces. When these beings encounter someone in need, they plant bulbs (literally and/or figuratively) to help that person heal. Each angel invited to this convention is a special blessing to Jane and Joe.

Out of the dead-looking bulbs, the flowers bloomed. Out of life-threatening illness, life-giving healing was born. Mystery. Miracle. The acts of God.

Four years later, Jane continues with maintenance treatment, has completed seminary with highest honors, and talks with love and passion about the tiny inner city church she serves. Then she speaks of that fall and winter and spring with a thoughtful smile and a mischievous sparkle in her eyes. "Bulb-planting angels. That probably sounds silly to other people. But all winter I looked out my window and knew the energy of all your love under the snow." My experience as a bulb-planting angel was transforming. I learned healing and discovered miracles.

Today I am recalling the words of the bishop as he talks to Mark, the young and dying priest. He speaks of learning what everyone must learn—"enough of the meaning of life to be ready to die." His words make me wonder what I still must learn and turn me to look at the learning that has reshaped my heart.

The community of bulb-planting angels changed my understanding of healing and of a hymn I had never liked. Natalie Sleeth had composed "Hymn of Promise" at the time of her husband's death. It proclaims that "in the bulb there is a flower" and speaks of the hidden promise of butterflies in cocoons. It ends with the proclamation of a resurrection in our death.[1]

In my theological orthodoxy, I have been uneasy talking about resurrection in the same breath as cocoons and butterflies, bulbs and flowers, winter and spring. It felt too "Greek" to me—as if a disembodied soul flows easily from this life into another, not really dying. No. Death is

106

death. Grief and loss and despair are real. Resurrection does not come "naturally" out of death in the way that butterflies come out of cocoons or bulbs turn into tulips or daffodils.

After experiencing Jane's healing and hovering around the flowers for a long time, something changed. Jane's healing did not come without the wisdom of exceptional doctors and newly developed medication. The tulip did not bloom without the flower's equivalent of DNA, along with water and sunshine, that pushes leaves and color up out of the hard ground. Nevertheless, I now knew both to be miracles, God's own miracles.

Ann Weems writes of those who "scoff at miracles," and so she wonders how they regard the birth of the Christ Child.

> For that matter,
> I don't know what they make of the birth of any child.[2]

For the one who looks with the eyes of faith, cocoons and butterflies, bulbs and flowers, winter and spring, the birth of any child—all speak of mystery, of miracle, acts of God. That is what Natalie Sleeth was writing. She ends each stanza affirming that the flower and springtime and resurrection are never revealed until the time is right and that is "something God alone can see."

This God who sees is the One with whom we are bound in relationship through Jesus Christ. God who sees is not one watching from afar, but is the One who has promised to be our covenant God, to be with us always. Our God's "seeing" is not "watching." God seeing is God acting in and with us. Whatever the healing and new life and resurrection—they are God's own acts, what some call miracles. They are not without the communities of bulb-planting angels. They are not without the skills of fine doctors and wise psychologists and gifted clergy. They are not without prayer and learning, practices and ritual. And—they are not ever without the seeing presence of our God.

Jane's healing and Linda's experience of new life, beside Natalie Sleeth's poetic wisdom, have reshaped a further constellation of images for me. I have come to see God's act of salvation in Christ as "healing." I have resisted that image. I thought it was not radical enough; it did not connote for me the discontinuity between our separation from God and the new relationship God created by the revolutionary act of coming to us in Christ. Then I learned healing. I learned through my own intimations of new life after the devastation I had known with Mark's death. That healing is nothing less than resurrection, God's miracle. I watched Jane discover she was unable to continue attending the classes she loved, my dear friend who never had failed to complete what she had begun. She was so weak, so sick. It was as Linda wrote in her journal:

> Pain and this disease have swept a million dreams into the ocean. Fighting it has robbed me of gusto and even small pleasures, eroding my sense of the sacred and meaningful in life.

Then healing. What could be more radical and discontinuous than to be brought from the edge of death into new life? That *is* salvation. That is what God is doing, moment by moment, miracle after miracle.

I have long puzzled over words about resurrection from two women whose lives and work I treasure. Sister Joan Chittister, reflecting upon Ecclesiastes 3:2, "a time to die," writes, "Death is resurrection unwanted."[3] Julia Esquivel, a Guatemalan teacher and poet, was forced into exile for many years because of her active resistance to the oppressive government of Guatemala. She chose for the title of her urgent poem about the struggles of her people: "They Have Threatened Us with Resurrection."[4] Resurrection once had a narrow meaning for me, but Chittister and Esquivel, my own journey, Jane's and Linda's stories, have transformed what the healing of resurrection means. Resurrection happens now. It happens as I leave behind parts of my life that needed to die. It happens as my dear congregation discovers a new beginning born of tragedy. It happens in a way for which I cannot ask, because I cannot even imagine it.

As I was completing this writing, it was that anniversary week in December when I remember standing by Mark's hospital bed. My two seminary colleagues with whom I work most closely brought me a gift that they hoped would be "a comfort in this season of memories."Anita and Julie did not know that the true meaning of their gift and their attentive care were in the book they offered. "Those who grace us in our grieving carry resurrection within them, giving flesh to the Wisdom born from the meeting of sorrow and joy."[5] I know resurrection. The community of faith and the wisdom of God bring resurrection—embodied this season in my dear colleagues who bring their gift of comfort.

As I was completing this writing, Linda called to say her disease was out of remission. Radical treatment has begun, and she writes,

I've battled this disease for a very long time. I mourn desperately. I hope that perhaps with another round of treatment the hurricane of this illness finally will pass over me. But treatment is only treatment. It cannot be an affirmation of life. There must be a personal affirmation that transcends issues of health and wellness, prognosis, treatment, &c. There must be an affirmation of life, not merely a battle against disease.

I want you to know that I go into this with a full commitment—not just body but spirit, the pieces held together by fierce desire, by faith in the future, in renewal and rebirth. I know that my power is not the last answer, and I have turned it over to God—but God gave me this spirit and this personality and this particular terrier way of being in the world and I intend to use it, believing it to be God's intent, too. Confidence has entered me and strength. I feel deeply happy.

l'chaiyim. life. to life.[6]

May God grace us all with this healing and resurrection, day after day, miracle after miracle.

NOTES

1. "Hymn of Promise," *The United Methodist Hymnal* (Nashville: The United Methodist Publishing House, 1997), number 707.
2. Ann Weems, *Kneeling in Bethlehem* (Philadelphia: The Westminster Press, 1980), page 49.
3. Joan Chittister, *There Is a Season* (Maryknoll, NY: Orbis Books, 1995), page 62.
4. Julia Esquivel, *Threatened with Resurrection: Prayers and Poems from an Exiled Guatamalan* (Elgin, IL: Brethren Press, 1994).
5. Jan L. Richardson, *In Wisdom's Path: Discovering the Sacred in Every Season* (Cleveland, OH: The Pilgrim Press, 2000), page 69.
6. E-mail to author from Linda Brown.